Memoir Of George Boardman Boomer

Mary Amelia Boomer Stone

Alpha Editions

This Edition Published in 2021

ISBN: 9789354489761

Design and Setting By
Alpha Editions
www.alphaedis.com
Email – info@alphaedis.com

EMOIR

OF

EORGE   OARDMAN   OOMER.

BOSTON:
PRESS OF GEO. C. RAND & AVERY.
1864.

TO

Mrs. Nancy McClellan Boomer,

THE BELOVED MOTHER OF THE SUBJECT OF THIS MEMOIR,

This Little Volume

IS AFFECTIONATELY INSCRIBED.

PREFACE.

⸺⊶⋇⊷⸺

WHEN, in compliance with the wishes of my brother's friends, I consented to prepare the following Memoir, it was with the expectation that I should find among his papers such material as would enable me to accomplish it with readiness and ease.

It was my privilege to share fully my brother's confidence throughout his entire life; and, in addition to this rich experience, I knew that he had amused himself from time to time by writing his own Autobiography, some of the pages of which he permitted me to look upon one beautiful summer's day, while we were sitting together in our father's house, during his last visit there before he became a soldier. This manuscript he destroyed. I also hoped for another resource, which has failed.

My brother had quite a reputation in the country towns as a public speaker, and in some instances wrote out his addresses. These were also destroyed, except some fragments of early preparations which have been introduced, although I know them to be very imperfect.

There seemed nothing left me but an indifferent journal, and a few letters, which are simple utterances of interest and affection, — the character of all his epistolary writing.

That I am compelled to ask any one to look at my brother's manly heart and industrious life through the medium of my poor pen, is a bitter disappointment ; still, I am grateful to Him who "controls all destinies" that I can bear even so feeble a testimony to the memory of one who gave me inexpressible joy, from the pure and gentle days of babyhood, to that hour when he lay cold in death on the far-off heights of Vicksburg.

In preparing the following Memoir, I have often been trammelled by the fear that I should not do my subject justice on the one hand, and on the

other, that I should trespass upon the boundaries
of good taste by speaking in such high terms of
my own kindred.

I desire to offer an apology for so long delaying
the accomplishment of this little volume. One
reason has been already assigned, — the lack of
material; the other is kindred to it, — the want
of time. In days like ours, when women must
work for their country while their loved ones fight
for it, private claims for time must be laid aside.

I am aware that this simple narrative has little
merit. It is only hoped that the reader will see
an earnest, honest, upright purpose in this life, so
poorly portrayed.

The world is more powerfully affected by one
true life than by many theories and principles.
The one is an ideal, the other a reality; the one
is a precept which appeals to the understanding,
the other an example which touches the heart,
strengthens the hopes, and kindles with new ardor
the purposes of the soul.

As this little work has been prepared exclu-
sively for private circulation, I feel assured that

those who read it will treat all its imperfections with forbearance and generosity. And here I cannot be restrained from acknowledging, not only the ready sympathy so tenderly offered to the bereaved, but also the sincere and eloquent tributes of esteem and love paid to him, who in his turn

> " has sunk to rest,
> By all his country's wishes blest."

M. AMELIA STONE.

CLEVELAND, June 25, 1864.

CONTENTS.

CONTENTS.

CHAPTER VIII.

CHAPTER IX.

CHAPTER X.

CHAPTER XI.

CHAPTER XII.

CHAPTER XIII.

CHAPTER XIV.

MEMOIR.

CHAPTER I.

BIRTH AND EARLY CHILDHOOD.

"God gives us love; something to love
  He lends us; but when love is grown
To ripeness, that on which it throve
  Falls off, and love is left alone."

TENNYSON.

HEN the voices of our loved ones die away, and we sit in the terrible silence of death, pressing closer and closer to our hearts remembrances of the dear images which have been torn from us, what myriads of fond recollections arise, — memories on memories, an exhaustless store. To the darkness of the past they reach, linked by many a hidden chain. At such a time, it is hard to touch with the coarse handling of words the dear objects which our hearts embalm. Brought into contact with another eye, the sacredness of the object is destroyed, the beautiful vision is disturbed, the "lovely organs" of that once dear life are marred.

2

If, in the full enjoyment of life, language is found inadequate to portray a just expression of our hearts' treasures, how much more so when we view them through the dark portals of death and the "bloom of eternity." Still, the heart cannot easily rest while the excellences of its loved ones lie forgotten; and if it is powerless to delineate the affluence of their virtues, those noble qualities of the soul which were apparent to all beholders may be perpetuated. Especially is this desired when, with a self-denial as grand as it is eloquent, our loved ones cheerfully sacrifice their all for their country.

It does not require the partiality of affection to throw a halo of glory around the names of those brave, unselfish men who have dared to stand up for liberty and right. Men in all ages, in all lands, have admired the heroic element. It develops such constancy, self-sacrifice, and endurance as to command the admiration of enemies, and the profoundest love of friends.

The magnanimous deeds of such men have been handed down to us in history, story, and song, by the sculptor's chisel and the painter's brush. Nations, too, have shown their appreciation of these representative men, and point with honest pride to the monuments which they have erected to keep their names and memories green in the hearts of future generations. If it is the privilege of all loyal-minded men to bear such record of those who have offered their lives upon the altar of liberty, there is united to the offering of those who claim a kindred with the honored dead, a higher pleasure in its being a tribute of affection. With such, the imagination can hardly be restrained from believing that those to whom we dedicate the homage of our hearts may be permitted in their heavenly home to recognize and enjoy the humble proofs we give that their toils, virtues, and sacrifices are held in sweet and unfading remembrance.

We are so keenly alive to the interests of the present moment, so anxiously stretching after the pursuit of future good, that we are prone to forget the sacrifices of the past. Yet human nature is not devoid of noble impulses, and the heart is capable of a gratitude true and generous.

Among the names of those who have followed the fortunes of our bleeding country, and who have died for it, is that of Brigadier-General Boomer, who was born in the town of Sutton, Worcester County, Mass., July 26, 1832.

GEORGE BOARDMAN BOOMER was the youngest child of the Rev. Job Borden Boomer, who, at

the time of his son's birth, had labored for nearly
twenty years in the church of which he was the
beloved pastor.

The advent of this child was hailed with great
joy by the two sisters and one brother of the
family, as well as by all the good people of the
parish, and many remarkable things were naturally predicted of the dear child in his days of
babyhood.

A visit to the parsonage, during the first few
weeks of the life of young Boomer, by the Baptist
missionary, George Boardman, decided his name;
and many were the silent prayers offered to the
wise Disposer of all things that the mantle of this
self-sacrificing Christian man might, in future
years, rest upon his infant namesake.

It scarcely needed the wise prognostications
of partial friends or of devoted parishioners to
foretell something uncommon even in the baby
infancy of little George. His early command of
words, his facility for combining them into sen-
tences, his power to group ideas and communi-
cate them, in connection with his large head
and intelligent eyes, were unmistakable signs
in the dawn of his future career.

The early surroundings and influences of this
child were of such a character as to refine the

taste and elevate the heart. The pure, healthful atmosphere of the country cradled and nourished his infant years, — the glorious country,

" Where every element conspires to bliss."

This home was in one of the lovely towns of New England, with its grand woods, its green hill-sides, smiling valleys, blooming orchards, pure pebbly brooks, its clear skies and bright stars.

The antique church upon the hill, which had stood there for many years, was a source of great wonder to the imagination of little George. The pews of the venerable building were square, its pulpit and galleries were high, and on either side of the sacred desk were paintings of angels, who, with their outspread wings, seemed to aid in raising the thoughts of the worshippers from sublunary to divine things.

At the left of the church, on the verge of the hill, stood the parsonage, adorned on one side by a large peach orchard, which, whether in fruit or flower, was a source of great delight to all the children of this happy home.

At the north lay a beautiful valley, watered by a quiet stream, which stretched on eastward, where it emptied itself into a little lake. Beyond this rose the hills again. These extended to the

2*

south, growing less and less distinct, until they
seemed resolved into woody slopes, at the feet
of which was spread a noble plain.

One particular feature in the landscape must
not be overlooked. This was a grove of tall pine-
trees, which had strange, mysterious voices for
a young imagination. There would the little boy
often wend his way, and listen for the footsteps
of the spirits who he firmly believed had an abode
there ; for this, in fact, was the spot where he
looked for the realization of the wonderful nursery
stories he had eagerly listened to of fairies and
genii. In after years this grove was loved for
far different reasons. It became beautiful indeed,
with its warm sunlight falling through the musical
trees, each branch of which seemed to give a
different note, though harmoniously

———" blent in one grand song of praise."

It was among these liberal gifts of nature, so
bounteously bestowed, that his early boyhood was
spent, loving most of all to be alone, and learning
by observation what is so often learned by asking
questions. This trait of his character, so early
developed, powerfully affected his subsequent life,
deepening the naturally mature tone of his mind,
and coloring his entire character.

He was precocious and premature, and often, in riper years, was heard to say that he knew no childhood. Not that he was querulous with other children or their sports. He was frank and happy in his disposition, thoughtful but not melancholy, very far from anything sullen or arrogant; but he seemed more happy when by himself, with a trifling toy, or some garden tools, basking in the sunshine, wading in the brook, or chasing the birds. In this way he was able to amuse himself, and this ability to draw upon his own resources was a prominent trait in his character throughout his entire life.

At the early age of three years he was allowed to follow his own inclinations in attending the village school; but it was not until a subsequent period that he at all distinguished himself as a scholar. When eight years of age, he was placed at the academy in Uxbridge, at that time one of the best institutions in the country, and it was there, at his first examination, that the quiet, thoughtful child made his first impression that he was a boy of bright, interesting talents.

There were many fine lads in that institution; and fond, ambitious parents awaited the first exhibition of the talents of their several sons

with true parental solicitude. The questions given
were answered with great credit to the *memories* of the young students, affording but little opportunity for one to vie with the other in
that respect. But leaving this department of
mind for one which required independent thought
and reflection, the little boy, with his careless
manner and unpretentious appearance, was not
only ready for an answer, but for the reasons
why; wholly unconscious, while arraigned before
this board of critics, replying to their questions
and cross-questions, of the complimentary verdict
that awaited him.

At that period he displayed but trifling ambition
for study, knew nothing of the spirit of rivalry,
cared little for a task, and applied no particular
energy to it. Still his lessons were well learned
and understood, — an unceasing wonder to all who
were familiar with his apparently indolent habits. With a retentive memory, and an ability
to grasp the reasons of things, the conclusions
were self-evident.

It was objected by his parents at that time
that he should commence the study of Latin, on
the ground that he was too young to comprehend
it, and that the task would be too difficult; but

his teacher, who understood his capacities better,
overruled the matter, and, after a few faithful
efforts, the dry Latin seemed to yield to his will
as easily as his more simple studies.

CHAPTER II.

SCHOOL-DAYS.

T was during this interesting period that young Boomer's heart opened and expanded into friendship. Those happy school-days furnished his first friend; and though only for a brief space of early boyhood did their paths lead in the same direction, yet so strong was the impression made upon his affections, so bright was the radiance which this early love spread over his whole being, that through his entire life no other friend seemed so dear. It was interesting to watch the sweet sympathy of these two little friends, Sammy and George. Their instinctive love for each other was so true, that they cared little to understand or analyze their emotions, so be that they could sit together at school, read from the same book, and be *alone* together out of school, — always kind and affectionate one to the other, and nobly defending each other from every injury or aspersion.

This incident was one of the most important events of Mr. Boomer's life. It was like the planting of good seed in good soil, and bore rich fruit. In his boy days the effect of such sympathy was expansive and exhilarating; he grew thereby. The influence of this human affection sweetened all his pursuits, duties, and pastimes, and as he advanced to manhood its truth and fidelity armed him against many a hard blow hurled by the misanthrope and sceptic against what is faithful in the human heart.

Scarcely more than a year of this happy boy-life was spent, ere the Rev. Mr. Boomer removed his residence to the town of Brookfield, and the two little friends were obliged to part, never again to renew the intimacy of that first sweet intercourse. This separation of the two boys extended to different pursuits in life, different scenes, far different homes and avocations. They seldom met, and were not correspondents; but always in life Mr. Boomer proved faithful to his early friend, and after his death such proofs of his attachment were found as must affect the heart.

Although but few of his papers or manuscripts were preserved, having been destroyed by his own hand, yet the first letter he received from this friend was found carefully folded away, bear-

ing on its worn single page a record that twenty
years had not obliterated the deliciousness of that
early, pure affection, which first awoke within
him the noblest emotions of his heart, and by
its truth had sweetened all the loves and friendships of his life.

That noble instances of friendship have existed
from "the cradle to the grave," is a fact indisputable. These are " divine applications, and are
but the rights of virtue with itself." But in
most instances the lives of these persons have
more or less commingled in mature years, after
the character had shaped itself into manhood or
womanhood. We instinctively look for something
tangible in a friend, — some threads of a nature
which we can naturally interweave with our
own ; but an attachment born in childhood, expanded in mature years by the impression only
of extreme youth, must owe its development to
something pure and true in the nature of the man
or woman with whom it is found.

The four succeeding years of his life were
spent in the beautiful village of East Brookfield,
where he had the same opportunity to enjoy the
loveliness of nature that was afforded him in the
place of his birth. Scarcely had the new pastor
established himself with his congregation, ere

his bright little boy, sitting in the front pew with a careless air and merry countenance, was the observed of all, and much attention was given to the child.

The older gentlemen of the parish would question him on subjects far beyond his years, and upon matters in which they were concerned, to hear his original, independent answers; and it was an interesting sight to see groups of people gathered around the church-porch, discussing the important arguments of the sermon with this young boy in the midst of them.

During his residence in that place the young people of the community formed themselves into a society for mutual improvement. They issued a paper, which was read at their gatherings. Young George felt that he could not allow his capacities of ten years to remain dormant while such a field of mental effort was suggested to him; so, calling the little boys of his own age together, they organized themselves into a society, based upon the same plan which was adopted by their seniors.

Some fragments remain of these early efforts. The following tribute to his native State contains quite an element of patriotism for one so young:—

3

"The history of Massachusetts is deeply interesting, interwoven as it is with every political or moral event that has transpired since the settlement of North America. She was first in the field for the defence of the homes of New England against the murderous tomahawk of the savage foe; the first in all the wars in which the mother-country was engaged on this continent, and the leader in that glorious struggle for the achievement of our national independence.

" Within her borders and by her citizens was kindled the flame which resulted in the entire separation of the colonies from the parent state and the formation of this mighty republic.

" The first acts of the Pilgrim fathers was to establish churches and school-houses, the result of which may be seen at the present time in the intelligence, enterprise, and morality of her citizens.

    .   .   .   .

" She abounds in thriving towns and villages. Public schools on every hand, seminaries of learning, hospitals, asylums, manufactories, public works, railroads, give ample proof of the industry, zeal, public spirit, and perseverance of her inhabitants."

Up to this period the boy-life of young Boomer had been one of uncommon sunshine. Time passed in a grand holiday with his pet dog or cat and his books. He seemed perfectly happy; but, probably in consequence of reading beyond his years, a new spirit was evidently awakening within him, his eye grew stronger, his step firmer, an occasional restlessness developed itself in his manner, and he begged to be sent away to school,—a wish which was gratified by his being placed at the academy at Attleborough, Massachusetts, the residence of his brother-in-law, Hon. John Daggett.

While pursuing his studies here, he made rapid progress; his ambition was stirred; the school was advantageous; and, added to that, he could not but reap great benefit from coming in contact with the highly cultivated mind of his brother-in-law, Mr. Daggett.

These school-days bore the first evidences of mental discipline, which served the desired purpose of awakening more and more the thirst for study. He seemed also to be roused by the first impulses of manhood, to feel how much there was in life, "how brief man's earthly span," and how precious the moments were as they passed.

A few months subsequent he was placed at the Worcester Academy; and the following record of his appreciation of that precious gift to man, time, written at this period, was found among his papers : —

" Time is God's great gift to his erring children, and next to the great concerns of the soul there is nothing for which we should entertain so high a regard.

. . . .

" Of all the losses which man may sustain, there are none so great, so grievous to be borne, as the loss of time. Not wealth, for that can be recovered ; not reputation, grievous as that may be, for that may be redeemed ; not friendships, for they are always changing ; — but time, once lost, is lost forever ; it passes away, never to have another resurrection, and is entombed with the centuries of the past.

" It behooves all right-thinking men to seize upon the hours as they fly, and with eager hand and watchful eye gather up the atoms of knowledge which each fleeting moment brings.

" Greatness consists not in loud-sounding titles, or in unbounded rule. He is greatest, and his sway most extensive, who discharges ably the duties assigned him by a wise Providence, who fulfils with fidelity all the requirements made of

him by the laws of his being, who bravely stems
the torrent of public wrong and private misfortune, and who, with undaunted spirit, resolves that
all his powers shall be so used as to honor the
great Author of all good. The task may be often
difficult and the labor hard, but the attainment is
sure, if but the time is industriously used; and
if the toil is heavy and the progress slow, the
reward will be the greater."

The first months of these school-days seemed
the very acme of happiness to young Boomer.
Filled with all the ardor of youth, impressed with
an unflinching desire not to study merely but to advance, enthusiastic to a fault, resolute in his plans,
sanguine for the future, he naturally looked directly forward, and saw only a straight road, along
which he felt strong enough to walk, defying any
crooked lines which might appear, and battling
with the "lions in the way."

These hopes were not all visionary. His prospects were truly flattering, as the institution was
one which had received considerable attention
from Mr. Boomer's relatives, and had a particular
interest for the sons of clergymen. Some of the
teachers were personal friends, and stood ready to
help the poor boy who was ready to help himself.

3*

There was no lack of personal effort on the part
of this young student, as he could and did help
himself; this was his ambition. Free in body and
mind, unfettered by disappointments or forebodings,
his mental vision fed upon the goodly prospect
which hope held out to him as a not far-distant
possession.

This state of mind, with his natural capacity to
master books, enabled him to go on with his
studies at a rapid pace; and at that time there
was little reason to doubt that he would be able
to enter upon his college course much younger
than most lads, and with comparatively less effort.

Nor were these days wholly given to books. He
was fond of his pen, and found time, aside from
its ordinary use in study, to indulge his fancy in
writing a little romance, descriptive of the early
development of chivalry among one of the German
tribes.

This story introduces, with apparent truthful-
ness, the gross immoralities, superstitions, and vices
of the world's history at that period, and depicts
in glowing colors the magnificent institution of
chivalry in its youth, softening and purifying the
degraded condition of that barbarous age.

He loved, too, the debate, and became one of its
warmest champions; was bold and fearless in say-

ing what he thought was right; could not endure that truth should be imprisoned in some "cloister of the mind" for fear of disastrous consequences. No one, as boy, youth, or man, had a greater abiding conviction of the power of truth, rightly wielded, than he, and he looked upon those who refused to use so potent a weapon as being possessed of a weak and cowardly spirit.

A circumstance illustrative of this trait of his character occurred in connection with the school at that time. The young gentlemen of the institution, in laying their plans for improvement and mental culture, decided upon inviting Theodore Parker, who had at that time attained the zenith of his glory, to lecture for them. This plan was greatly opposed, not only by some of the teachers, but by the patrons of the institution and the parents of the young men. Boomer took firm ground in defence of Mr. Parker's lecture : —

"Was there not enough of the true, noble, and praiseworthy in Mr. Parker to afford a healthful stimulus for young men? Must one, of necessity, imbibe his errors in listening to his truths? Mr. Parker was one of the great men of the age, and had by his industry and zeal in study made almost incredible attainments. Truly," he stoutly main-

tained, " Mr. Parker's appreciation of the value of
a day, a week, a month of time, is a virtue of so
high an order as to commend him to the attention
of every young student who wishes to accomplish
something in life."

It was during the early part of these school-days
that the election campaign of President Taylor
agitated the country. This circumstance directed
his mind more fully to our national affairs, the
responsibilities of each individual citizen, the
political economy of our country, its wonderful
resources, and the necessity of education as a
means of developing them, as the following pas-
sages will indicate : —

" The mission of our country is a great one.
She has and will in the future act a noble part in
the progress of the world's history.

" A cursory survey of the extent of our territory, reaching from the Atlantic to the Pacific, its
eastern and western boundary of oceans, with its
chain of cold lakes on the north, and the tropical
gulf on the south, embracing splendid varieties of
soil and climate, affording ample scope for the
agriculturist, the mechanic, the mineralist, etc.,
— what a vast theatre for the mind to act upon!

"The call is for industry; and industry, the true basis of American character, has, in its earnest simplicity, made our nation more grand, even in its extreme youth, than any of the proud realms of the Old World, though encircled with the accumulated strength of centuries.

"In days gone by the cultivation of the practical, physical sciences did not receive that rank as a power to civilize the world that it now holds, and that it must hold in our country to make that use of her untold resources, the like of which has never been equalled in a nation's wealth.

"The boy, the youth, the man, has always presented to his understanding some stimulus for labor, some way of bettering his condition in life, which in our country never ends in its aspirations with anything less than an independence,— independence, that innate but lawful feeling which thrills the heart of every true man.

"This is the real element of our greatness. Such opportunities for personal success stir within the heart an activity which must develop our fair country as no other country has been; and this, at the present day, should be the prime object of education.

"This devotion to physical science will not degrade or lower the mind of man; on the contrary,

it is that beautiful, harmonious machinery which
will work out those national characteristics, of
which, as citizens of the United States, we justly
feel a pride."

In the early stages of this campaign, Mr. Boomer's conservative nature was quite aroused by the
movements of the Anti-slavery party. He dili-
gently studied and gave much reflection to their
operations, and left some records of the same : —

"We live in an age of revolutions ; the whole
world is a vast theatre of change. What yesterday was powerful and seemingly irresistible, to-
day lies prostrate in the dust. Europe is strug-
gling with the iron grasp of despotism, and substi-
tuting, as far as possible, the forms of republican-
ism. Kings and emperors are bowing before the
inflexible will of the people, and consternation fills
the minds of tyrants.

"But this revolutionizing spirit does not confine
itself to Europe or any other portion of the world.
Republican America desires a change. Yes; and
she needs a change. But what is the change she
needs ?

"She is on the eve of an important presidential
election. There are within her borders two great

national parties which divide her citizens and her country, and which ever have divided it. These two parties are widely separated by great questions of national policy; but one of them ever has been, and ever must be, in power. There is, also, at the present time a third party, not national, but geographical, which withdraws itself from the national parties on sectional principles, and terms itself the Free-soil or Anti-slavery party, claiming to be the only representative of those principles.

"If this be so, if they can be accomplished in no other way, and if there are not other principles of as much or more importance to the welfare of our great nation which they do not recognize,— if they are honest in their own pretensions, and show to the world that they have means for fulfilling the same, then they are entitled to respect.

"But in order to accomplish their professed objects and win the respect of the country, what should be the character of this party? What sort of men should compose it?

"Certainly it ought to consist of men whose whole lives have been devoted to the objects professed, at least its leaders should be such; and most assuredly the man they hold up to the people of this country as candidate for the chief office of the nation, through whom they expect

to accomplish all their designs, should be one
who has devoted his whole life, soul, and energies to the cause of freedom. But, I ask, is such
the case ? Will any of Mr. Van Buren's most
sanguine partisans affirm, with sincerity, that his
life has been devoted to the cause of freedom,
or that the least portion of it has been? Was it
devoted to such an object when, in the presence
of assembled thousands, at Washington, he gave
his solemn oath that then and forever he would
devote his energies to the continuation of slavery
in the District of Columbia? Was it when he
gave his vote for the bill allowing southern post-
masters to search the mails? — an act so odious
that, had it passed the American Congress, the pro-
ceedings of the very convention which nominated
Mr. Van Buren for the office of President must
have been excluded from the larger portion of our
Union. Was it when he sent the armed schooner
Grampus to one of our neighboring States, with
orders to seize and carry into captivity fifty-three
kidnapped Africans, then free by the laws of
the land, that Mr. Van Buren demonstrated his
love for liberty? Was it, too, when, in 1840 (although he at first opposed the expediency of the
measure), he acquiesced in the foul and disas-

trous plot of annexation, and gave it, and the consequent war, his firm support?

"A few weeks since we were told by Mr. Van Buren's friends and supporters that he has repented — that he is a changed man; but at the same time *he* is informing us that these acts of his life are a consolation to him, and, were he placed in similar circumstances, he should do the same again; and even in the attempt of some of his friends to make this discrepancy plausible, he frankly says, in his letter of acceptance to the Buffalo convention, 'that the well-meaning gentlemen were mistaken.'

"This is the man who is the champion of freedom! this is the martyr of liberty! and this is repentance! Truly, if this be so, the revolutions of the age must have changed the meaning of terms.

"But this party is composed of those who profess all kinds of principles, all kinds of pretensions, with as many methods of carrying them out. There are true Democrats, who will here fully represent their interests; true Whigs, who would not support the nominee of their own party, but see here the better path for maintaining their own honor; true Abolitionists, who also have here perceived the just course for them to pursue; and Mr. Van Buren is true to them all.

4

"Perhaps this may be the case; but if so, let him remain in his truth; let him derive consolation from it. The people of this country do not wish to change his position; they have changed it once, and they will never change it again.

"But the people of America do desire a change. They need a change; for the miscalled democracy have held the reins of government for the last four years with sad results. We are this day feeling the effect of what they have done, namely, the annexation of slave territory; an unjust war with a sister republic; the addition of more territory; the constant exercise of the odious veto power, for which act, in the monarchy of England, the last monarch who dared exercise it was punished with the scaffold. We have also upon our hands a heavy national debt; we have unsafe rivers and harbors; and, in fine, a general depression of business, ruinous to the great and vital interests of our country.

"Certainly, then, we need a change; and to effect it we must not place a man in the presidential chair who cherishes and maintains the very principles we wish to repudiate. No; we must place some one there who will carry out the principle of no more war, no more vetoes, no more annexation; but, on the other hand, a sound national currency, a well-directed system of internal improvements, the protection of our home industry; and, in short, the spirit of our great, good, and glorious Constitution must be maintained as it was by our earlier Presidents, Washington, Adams, and Jefferson. These are the principles of the Whig party, and these are the principles which they hope to secure to their country in the coming presidential election."

CHAPTER III.

DISAPPOINTMENT.

T is evident that Mr. Boomer had set his standard high, and was ambitious to excel; or, as he used to say, "he wanted to be a man," — not an automaton, an idler, but to accomplish something in the world; and he seemed, indeed, at this period to be travelling the highway to success. The golden apple was in view, but not to be reached until other and harder lessons were learned than any that had previously been given him.

Hitherto he had been an easy student; the great lessons of disappointment and self-discipline had not been found upon the pages of his book of life. Their hard though useful lessons, so common to the lot of all mankind, came, perhaps, rather early in his life; but he was not too young to feel their bitterness, — a bitterness which none but God knew.

When finishing his preparatory course, with the goal in sight, he began to suffer from pain

in his eyes; but thinking them only overtasked,
he allowed them a few months' respite, and commenced using them with renewed zeal.

This trial was followed by another disappointment. Still, as he gave no intimation of yielding
his design to pursue a course of study, his friends
urged him to give up, for a year, the idea, and
engage in some healthful out-door occupation, as
he was then very young to enter upon his col-
legiate course. An opportunity soon presented
itself for travelling in the northern parts of Vermont and New Hampshire, which he gratefully
accepted. For a time this disappointment seemed
only "a blessing in disguise," affording a delightful exchange from the close confinement of the
school-room to the beautiful scenery of the Green
Mountains. Nature often proves to be man's best
teacher, — "she unseals the eye, illumes the mind,
and purifies the heart."

Added to these kindly influences was the in-
vigorating effect of the climate, which imbued
him with fresh strength, and he began to feel that
the time he was destined to spend in that delightful country, opening to him a new field of interest,
was only designed as an additional preparation
for the glowing future of his hopes, — always keeping in view the end he had proposed.

4*

The following extracts from letters give some views, or thoughts, during his stay in that interesting region : —

"CHIPMAN POINT, August 19, 1850.

"DEAR SISTER: As it regards my health, I have been in a country where, if careful, in the ordinary course of events, it could be scarcely otherwise than good, for which I have great reason to be thankful, while so many are being daily cut off by the fearful ravages of cholera.

"You are aware that after I left home I remained some time at Bellows Falls, or made it my rendezvous. The country around there is pleasant, although in warm weather the village, in some parts, is unhealthy because low.

"Some of the time I stopped at Ludlow, twenty-six miles north of Bellows Falls. This place is situated at the foot of Mt. Holly, and is delightfully cool and pleasant, being shaded with trees, while the mountain towers several thousand feet above it, although its base is upon very high land.

"I left Ludlow the 10th. The scenery along the route was most charming, especially among the Green Mountains. But this is by far the most beautiful spot I have seen since I have been in Vermont. It is four miles only from Fort Ticonderoga, so renowned in the history of our country in that day that tried men's souls, — which place I have visited, and there beheld the fast-disappearing walls within whose pale our forefathers offered their life's blood as a sacrifice upon the shrine of liberty.

"There is a rest, a repose, a charm in this country that is inexpressible; a happiness that is subdued by the all-pervading sense that you are surrounded by 'dim shadows' of the great Omnipotent; evidences of the Divine Worker are seen on every hand. The green earth sends up its incense from every mountain-side."

"How much the contemplation of these noble traces of God's work, —

'In all these fair forms I see,'

awes the soul, and makes it sink into insignificance! Yon proud mountains standing there in their wealth of green, girded with strength as with an armor, how glorious they are!

"Yet man is greater than yonder mountains. He bears, and he only, the image of the great builder, God. He was 'made a little lower than

the angels,' and has the power given him to rule
and reign over these everlasting hills. How
wonderful, then, is man!"

In after years, when prostrated with the de-
bilitating effects of a southern climate, he longed
for the sweet valley of the Otter Creek, with the
reverential spirit that seemed to rest upon all
the hills and glens of that poetical region; — a
wish he always gratified as often as he could
command the time.

After a year thus spent he returned to his
books again, with his mind and heart all in fine
condition for the accomplishment of his long-
expected plans; but bitter the decree, — the nerves
of his eyes were so affected that they could not
be used for consecutive study, for years.

He was at this time seventeen years of age,
with a mind remarkably mature, uncommonly dis-
ciplined, and well stored with general information.
All his wishes and plans and thoughts had been
given to study. Hopeful in his disposition, he
had not dreamed that such an apparently slight
difficulty could triumph over so healthy a body
which contained so strong a will.

This was a crushing event, the great sorrow of
his life, and at that time bowed him to the earth.

It seemed too much for him to bear. Life, *his*
life, was denied him. The medium through which
he looked into the future was dark, the road he
had designed to walk was closed to him forever.
What could he do? Whither could he turn?
Ardent, earnest, enthusiastic, with the soul of a
poet, how could he yield all his tastes, his own
heart's longings, for what seemed to him, at that
time, the wearisome pursuits of business men?

He was poor, and knew the necessity of personal effort. He felt its dignity, and gloried in
the fact that every man was most a man when
carving his own name in the world; but he had
read his future through the discipline of study,
and was not prepared to make so great a sacrifice as to abandon it.

This was a struggle, a terrible conflict, which
lasted for months. He battled against his own
reason, against the testimony of medical men,
against the advice of those who loved him best;
but the strength of his purposes was such that
it was not easy to surrender what he had so
determinedly marked for his earthly career; and
when at last he saw the folly of wasting time in
regrets, and felt how important it was that he
should acquire a knowledge of business, it was

that he might ultimately, in some way, gratify his early ambition for study.

Notwithstanding this severe shock, this great trial of his character, yet the important fact of life, with all its relations and connections, stood out before him, and this discipline, which called for patience and endurance, so requisite for the future struggle, was not unheeded.

In the winter of 1851 Mr. L. B. Boomer, an elder brother, and Mr. A. B. Stone, a brother-in-law, entered upon an extensive business of bridge-building throughout the Western and Southwestern States. The head-quarters of this new firm was established at Chicago, Ill.; yet some important contracts in Missouri made it necessary that they should open an office in St. Louis; and it was in the charge of this department that Mr. Boomer first entered upon his business career, at the age of nineteen years.

This was a great event in his history, and fraught with many forebodings. He had been reared in the atmosphere of religious sentiment, and the associations of his home had been such as to stir within him a loving humanity, sanctified by the holy convictions of religious truth. He had always preferred the quiet fireside of his

home, by the side of his mother, to the common
pastimes of boyhood ; and to make the great
change, to launch into the world of men, so far
from all that had hitherto surrounded him, to
make for himself a new world, was an unan-
swered problem.

After he had decided the question, to go or
not to go, in his own mind, he submitted its
final decision to his mother, whose judgment he
had always trusted, and who, at great cost, with
many prayers and tears, bade her son depart,
trusting that the protecting power of an all-wise
God would do more towards guiding his steps
aright than earthly father or mother.

In leaving the home of his childhood for one
of his own making, Mr. Boomer was manly and
full of courage. But that he had given thought
and reflection to the subject, and that with such
thoughts and reflections success would certainly
crown his efforts, is evident by the following
truthful ideas : —

" But why quarrel with my fate ? Nay, why
quarrel with God's plans, so much better than
mine ? I have my own individual life, my personal existence, with all the thoughts, feelings,
wishes, and emotions of a man. Therefore I am

not poor, I am not impoverished. On the other
hand, I have great possessions, — more than I can
possibly comprehend.

"But this great wealth of life and being impose
upon me responsibilities. My physical and mental
existence are, in a great measure, at my own dis-
posal. I am to work with them; and if I refuse
to bear the yoke in my youth, what can I expect
to be the condition of my mental and moral
character in mature years?

"There are many weeds which spring up in
the garden of the mind, and if the soil is fertile,
strong labor will be required to eradicate them.
Man is a strange commixture of good and ill, and
he is often short-sighted in his tendencies to good.
In my disappointment, then, I must not presume
to defy my fate. I must yield my own will when
it seems plainly overruled by the great Omnipotent; for I cannot lift the veil which links my
present existence with my earthly future, leading
on, as it does, to the eternal years.

"Man's thirst for knowledge is often another
name for ambition, a disguise for power, which
degenerates into the weakest vanity, and ruins
the whole character; whereas the truly great is
often made so by the discipline arising from con-

tending with the greatest difficulties and sur-
mounting the greatest obstacles.

"There is a philosophy, as weak as it is unjust,
awarding no true greatness to moral heroes; passing coldly by those noble souls who do not find
'their paradise under the shadow of swords.'

"Thank Heaven there are but few such philosophers; the world is more just, and places, generally, a better, truer estimate upon the grandeur
of moral actions.

'The soul that can render an honest and a perfect man
Commands all light, all influence, all fate.' "

CHAPTER IV.

A NEW HOME.

O N the month of February, 1852, Mr. Boomer arrived at the city of St. Louis.

He describes the morning of his arrival there as dark and gloomy. He was weary with a long journey, having travelled by way of Cincinnati and Louisville, and met with several detentions on the way.

He was emphatically a stranger, with a single letter of introduction, — a stranger to his new duties, which imposed upon him responsibilities far beyond his years, — and with the burden of his disappointment still upon his heart. These circumstances made the issue of this unsolved problem doubtful.

Of his journey to his new home, he says: —

"My anticipations concerning the West have not been disappointed, neither have they been precisely realized; in fact, it is different from what I have supposed, without being worse.

"The thriving and fresh appearance which all Western towns are supposed to possess is in many instances sadly wanting, I assure you, and, in some cases, not only the appearance, but the essence of business is deficient. This is particularly the case with the river towns, many of which, both on the Ohio and Mississippi, have been laid out on a supposition that they were to become places of great importance, and failing that, have very decidedly an old and dilapidated look. The river towns of Indiana, Southern Illinois, Missouri, and some of the Kentucky towns, are of this class, with a few exceptions, of course.

"The general appearance of the land, or the scenery, on the Ohio, after leaving Louisville, is very monotonous, as is the case for about two-thirds the distance between Cincinnati and the latter place. The land is not always low, but always in tables or flats, and invariably covered with an old and luxuriant-looking growth of wood, commonly water-oak.

"The scenery on the Mississippi, from the mouth of the Ohio four hundred miles south, as that is all I could vouch for, is alternately bluff and flats, and is rather agreeable, that is, when the weather is such that you can view it from the deck of a boat. The flats are extremely low, and, in high water, flooded; but you will, in almost all instances, find opposite these the bluffs. In going up the river, some time since, I had the good fortune to descry a large fire on one of these, extending nearly a mile on the river, and it was truly a magnificent sight. Viewed from a distance it appeared like some vast fireworks."

After a few days Mr. Boomer located himself at the Planters' House, fixing his place of business directly opposite. This first step being accomplished, the next thing for him to decide was his place of public worship, which was the Second Baptist Church.

This step brought him into contact with William M. McPherson, Esq., who took at once a great interest in the young stranger; and occupying, as he did, a prominent position in the city, both in business and social relations, he offered him such kindness and attention as to forever fill Mr. B.'s heart with gratitude and love.

The following letters will give some idea of his first impressions of Missouri, and also of the manner in which his time was spent: —

" St. Louis, March 9, 1852.

" DEAR SISTER : This morning I came in from
the country, where I had been into the interior of
the State one hundred and twenty-five miles. My
journey was not altogether pleasant, although, to
a person disposed to take it so, there was plenty
of romance; but for my part I was disposed to
make a reality of living on what the natives call
'hog and corn,' sleeping six or eight in a room,
getting lost in the woods twice in a day, and going without clean clothing for a fortnight. The
beauties of the country are said to be inconceiv-
able; they were to me, as I dared not look about
very much, for fear I should fall off my horse;
therefore I am unable to describe anything which
would interest you.

" Since my return to the city we have had snow,
which fell last Sabbath and remained till Wednesday. Since then it has been as warm and pleasant as September, and the frost is nearly out of the
ground. I think we are exactly at the point where
the warm and cold climates are contending for the
supremacy; and we have abundant evidence that
neither obtains it for a long time. Nevertheless,
climate aside, St. Louis is a fine city. There is a
tone of health, vigor, and enterprise about it that
I did not expect to find; an order and propriety

5*

about all the customs of business, etc., which it is
charming to see.

"I am very well, except a something like bron-
chitis, that prevents me from singing. In fact I
have been obliged to stop altogether, as the least
effort affects me very sensibly. I regret it, for
I was flattering myself on a great improvement
in that way. At least 'one more unfortunate'—
bad eyes, bad throat.

.   .   .   .

"You speak truly of the passion with which
many are carried away, that is, money-making, and
I shall be obliged to confess that I have some of it
myself; but I can assure you that, although it is
in some cases a sad failing, it is a very easy one
to fall into. I can say, however, that it is not my
only ambition to make money; and, in fact, I have
not much of any sort, and certainly would not
desire such ambition to destroy anything which
contributed to the enjoyments of true life.

.   .   .   .

A few weeks later he writes,—

"I am quite contented and happily situated;
have just moved my room to one of the pleasantest localities of the city,— an office room and
sleeping room connected. I have them furnished

with plain, good furniture, and you must imagine
that their appointments do me much credit, especially my private sitting-room, as a gentleman
yesterday said that he knew I would be a 'bachelor,' for the reason that I displayed so much taste
and order in the arrangement of my rooms.

"Here I have my piano, which you may think
a bit of extravagance, but it has this good moral
answer, of amusing me evenings. I shall be more
likely to stay at home, and as I cannot read, on
account of my eyes, I must have something to
keep me there during the long hours.

"I am also giving a part of every evening I
am in town to learning French. There are fine
opportunities of mastering the language here, and
it is much spoken in the best society. You are
aware that most of the original citizens of this
place were French, and being proprietors of real
estate at the time when the rapid growth of population and consequent rise of landed property
commenced, they were immediately constituted
the aristocracy of the place. Thus, in that society,
French was, and is still, very common.

"I have not yet made many acquaintances, and
do not intend to do so, as living with large circles
of acquaintance is a great consumer of time, and
necessarily expensive.

"My business goes on prosperously. It occupies me during the day; and in that I am content. In the evening I read a very little, think about it a good deal, play some, and, in fact, make the most use I can of my leisure hours."

Of the resources of his new home, either in city or country, Mr. Boomer said nothing for some time. This was a study, — a book which he was able to read at his own pleasure.

Whatever struggles he passed through during his early residence there, were known only to his own heart; but it soon became evident that he was determined to succeed in what he had undertaken, if by energy and perseverance he could accomplish it.

This being plunged into an entirely new atmosphere, coming into contact with a class of people whose customs and habits were strange to him, with the reputation of the new firm entrusted to his hands, as well as his own personal success to accomplish, without any one to lean upon, was, in the end, a great blessing. It drove him to his own resources, developed within him powers of which he had hitherto been unconscious, and trained him, by this sharp, healthy discipline, to energy, courage, decision, and self-confidence.

He says that there was enough in his business to absorb and interest, enough mental effort to plan and arrange, enough obstacles to overcome. The greatest difficulty to contend with was in gaining the confidence of the people. The habits of thought among the St. Louians were such as inclined them not to trust at once a young man of nineteen, and a stranger, with important business contracts. Mr. Boomer saw the justice of this, and felt that he must be guided by the strictest rules of honor, good sense, and propriety, and that time must develop his right to be trusted.

"The time will come," he said, "when, doubtless, I shall wish to turn the hand backward upon the dial of my life, and bid the years recede; but now, for my present convenience, I would like to put it forward.

"It is shocking for a man to be too young, and short too. Oh, combination of evils! I cannot impress upon the minds of these conservative people that I am the man who has in charge the building of bridges for the State of Missouri, although they are too well bred to say so; yet their countenances brand me with a significance that savors of Young Americanism.

"I am relieved, to-day, in having had the oppor-

tunity of boldly asserting my manhood. While
writing at my desk, a fine-looking gentleman
bowed himself into the office, and asked, ' Is Mr.
Boomer in now?' The clerk replied, 'Yes, sir,'
when I accordingly stepped forward.

"After exchanging the commonplaces of the
day, which, on his part, was done with rather a
puzzled air, he said, 'My business was with Mr.
Boomer, sir,' to which I replied that I should be
most happy to serve him; but he persisted, 'Are
you not Mr. Boomer's son?' 'Certainly, sir; my
father's name is Boomer, but as he is at this time
probably engaged in some parish duty in one of
the quiet towns of New England, your interview
cannot be with him."

The first months of his life here were spent entirely in his new business; all his energies were
absorbed in it; and, during that time, he wrote
little of what he was thinking or doing.

One delightful feature of his life was the study
of character. Some of its phases here were new,
and necessity as well as pleasure prompted him to
the task. On this subject, in after years, he said,
"As man is God's crowning work, as he possesses a spark of the divine, and as he has been
placed to have dominion over all inferior creation,

it seems to me that his character is the highest
study of this earth."

That he had some trials, and was sometimes
oppressed by them, will be readily seen from a
letter to his sister: —

"St. Louis, August 8, 1853.

"My sweet Sister : Your good letter was duly
and happily received. I grieve to hear you are so
unwell; but that is a poor consolation any time,
much more from one so far away.

"Should you allow me to advise you, I would
say, keep perfectly quiet, as though it was no
matter what happened. If able, ride out every
pleasant evening, and give yourself up to perfect
abandonment of ease and good cheer.

"You say the truth of our poor friend. How
unhappy all are who do not, as you have said,
know true happiness. We live either in the future
or the past, but too rarely in the present. No
matter how situated, something blights the vision
of happiness, and the restless mind is compelled
to long for it in the uncertain future, or regret
its absence in the venerated past, where time
gilds all enormity into virtue, and all misery into
romantic joy.

"In the stern, real present, in what can man say he enjoys life most? In himself or another? For my part, though situated as favorably in most respects as could be wished, and perhaps enjoying that situation as well as most would, I sometimes feel that it is an unhappy thing to live as the present moment directs, and, as I have said before, I either long for happiness in uncertain futurity, or regret its absence in the by-gone. In any event, everything tells me that all which concerns one's true happiness is within us, and the effort to increase that by prosperity is as vain as the expectation to crush it by adversity. I sometimes wish that I could live in some retired place, among the cool, green hills of Vermont, where quiet homes and nature's profound sublimity teach the true genius of enjoyment; and should fortune and circumstances permit, I intend there to fix a home.

"Do not imagine by this that I am discontented; but in one's sober moments, weary with a struggle, we can but think that a quiet home, with friends for associates, would be a rare exchange for the noisy, uncertain life which business men are compelled to lead. Perhaps, however, the difference with me consists in the fact that the one is present, the other anticipated.

"So we had better endeavor to do well as we are, and let the future reveal itself as we live on."

In the summer of 1853, Mr. Boomer made his first visit to New England. In anticipating this visit he was somewhat anxious for the result. He did not want to love the place of his birth the less, but if he would truly accomplish what he ought in life, his heart must love the scene of his labor the more.

A letter written to his sister, on returning, will show the sequel : —

"St. Louis, October 12, 1853.

"My dear Sister: After leaving you, I went directly to Boston, where I had the good fortune to find my dear friend W——, with whom I had an elegant time. I assure you I counted time by 'heart throbs.'

"From there I went to New York, where I met A—— and his wife, as I expected; from which place we started for home on the following Monday, — Miss P——, from Springfield, the two Belles and nurse, constituting quite a party.

"We were late all the way to Chicago (that is, the cars were), and of course there was a

6

continual and general depreciation of the management of railroads and steamboats *in toto.* For the first day we yielded to the general discomfort ; but finally, after some consultation, thought we would draw upon our philosophy, and rise above what seemed disagreeable ; and we were bound to believe at the end of our journey, and resolved that always in the retrospect we would believe, that we had enjoyed ourselves intensely all the way ; in fact, that the journey had been profitable as well as pleasant.

"It was a little uncomfortable to wait on the prairie for several hours, when we were hungry and our lunch-baskets empty ; still we had the pleasure of learning something of human nature in that country in the shape of two or three humble farmers ; and we also improved the opportunity of learning something of the manners of housekeeping as we passed along, our hunger in many instances overcoming our timidity. We also had to learn lessons of patience and endurance at hotels, where all was full, literally full.

"I was really pleased to get here, — it seemed like home when I first had a view of the city. This was a spontaneous feeling, and filled my heart with gladness, — that, as this must be my future abiding-place, I should have for it kindly emotions. It was pleasant, and all the country possessed the dark, rich appearance which the foliage and fields have here in summer, and, though not in material contrast with the North, yet it seemed to me uncommonly beautiful.

"Alas! how changed! One cold night came, and made sad work with the leaves, which bear now unmistakable signs of autumn. Besides, for the last three days it has rained, which always makes the city look like a prison, and feel like one, too, when cold."

No sooner did he see success dawning upon his future, and some of the waves of difficulty receding with which he had been stoutly baffling, than his old thirst for books revived again, which he immediately began to lay plans for indulging. "At least," he said, "I can collect a library; which will be in better taste, certainly, than throwing away my money upon trifles. Books upon one's shelves are very suggestive of literature, if one is only wise enough to conceal the fact that the contents have not got into his head."

Perhaps the first year of Mr. Boomer's residence in St. Louis was the happiest one of his life; for in that time he had succeeded in establishing for himself a reputation far beyond his years, or even his most sanguine expectations, and which he owed entirely to his own merits. Under his faithful management the business grew rapidly, and in consequence he was admitted as a partner in the firm.

Still he saw another enterprise in his future, that of his social position, which he was determined to win unaided save by his own efforts. This was not an easy matter to attain in an old aristocratic city like St. Louis. But Mr. Boomer was not long in finding his way to the most refined and polished circles of social life. One of his friends, in reference to this subject, says that his entrance into society, without the patronage of friends, introductions, or by letters, was such as had never come under his observation before; but his manliness, frankness, and integrity, combined with modesty and good sense, a warm-hearted, genial nature, an amiable disposition, which was just and appreciative, won for him universal esteem, and not many months passed before he became a beloved favorite.

After the lapse of a year or more, Mr. Boomer began to recover the use of his eyes, which he greedily appropriated to his darling pursuits. He laid out a course of historical reading, reviewed his Latin and Greek under a master, and although these plans were often interrupted by journeys into the country, and frequent sickness, from which he suffered in consequence of a change of climate, yet they were never abandoned.

CHAPTER V.

HILE pursuing the necessary details of his business, travelling about the State, always willing to drop the distasteful for the agreeable, Mr. Boomer's attention was attracted by the beautiful scenery of the Osage River. His love of the artistic and poetical gave a peculiar charm to that part of the scenery which bore no traces of man's handiwork.

The native forests which covered the winding banks of this beautiful stream were, in many instances, untouched by the woodman's axe. These he could not sufficiently admire; and in the year 1854 he undertook an enterprise which afforded ample scope for his love of romance.

It seemed expedient, in carrying out successfully the bridge-building of the firm, that they should manufacture their own lumber; and for this purpose, mainly, Mr. Boomer bought of Government a township of heavily wooded land, eligibly located on the banks of the Osage River, fifteen miles from its mouth.

A saw-mill was immediately erected, and with such good success, — so great seemed the facilities of manufacturing, and the location of the place was so fine for a residence, — that he conceived the idea of building a little town, on the genuine New England principle, as far as compatible with the manners and customs of the people, stimulating thereby, if possible, the country towns to greater internal progress.

This decision being made, his next step was to give his town a name. In vain did his friends urge that he should perpetuate his own name upon the archives of the State; but, seizing upon a common tradition of that region, that an old man by the name of Castle once lived in the cave of a rock upon a high bluff across the river, he called his town "Castle Rock;" although the place is at present more commonly known by the name of "Boomer's Mills."

Some one has said that the glory of a State depends upon the nature of its lands and the spirit of its men. But Mr. Boomer discovered another ingredient in the resources of his adopted State, which was the character of its climate. He said that the State of Missouri had internal resources, which, if well developed, would add not only to its own glory, but to that of the whole Union. She had fertile valleys, noble rivers, minerals in great abundance and variety; she had splendor of scenery and richness of climate; but the question unsolved was, What would the spirit of her men do with their internal wealth?

That she failed of the enterprise which was the proud boast of the free States, and that she was far behind these free States for the reason of depending upon slave labor, was a stubborn fact; and the worst feature of the fact was, that the masses were not sufficiently intelligent to realize it.

Mr. Boomer was sometimes accused by friends in Massachusetts of sympathizing with the South on the subject of slavery. He certainly did not approve of some of the abolition movements of his native State; but as it was not his nature to contend, — always kind and charitable of the opinions of others, — he quietly maintained his own views upon this subject until the riot in Boston, occasioned by resisting the fugitive-slave law, brought out some of his sentiments. He believed that law should be held supreme, even if it be unjust, and its authority maintained in all cases, however painful, in some instances, the results may be; and that stern adherence to its sacredness, as law, is our only surety of any government.

"That he believed in slavery," he said, "was a libel. He had seen slavery as it existed in Missouri, and was near enough to those localities where it existed in a worse form, to judge for himself; and every pulsation of his heart was in sympathy with the slave.

"But here it is, and here it has been. It was left us by our forefathers, and is a constitutional right. The question is, how we are to dispose of this evil; — how can this dark spot be erased from our otherwise unstained land? I believe it must be by gradual emancipation. To set all our slaves free without any preparation, would require at once the power of the bayonet; we should be plunged into civil war.

"You are unjust toward the South, looking upon aggravated cases of cruelty; you judge all holders of slaves guilty of the same enormities, and brand them with epithets unworthy Christianity or humanity.

"This institution is deplored by many of the really intelligent in this State, and in other slave States, with a sincerity that the North will not appreciate. They see the progress which the free States make in agriculture, trade, and the mechanic arts around them; they see plainly how *they* fail of this prosperity by slave labor; and they realize, far better than the North can, the corrupting influence which it has upon the white population. There is no difference of opinion between us on the *moral* right of holding our fellow-men in bondage, none; but there is a wide difference, in my opinion, about the mode of removing this evil. I deprecate the lawless abolition movement of your State; a movement regardless of law, order, society, or government; advocated by men who would willingly sacrifice all our civilization, all our intelligence, all our most sacred social institutions, to carry out the single idea with which they are infatuated — of liberating the slave.

"You say such is not *public* sentiment, and can do no harm; which, to a certain extent, is true, and to a certain extent is not true.

"Could such traitorous opinions proceed from these higher-law men publicly, if there was no public to listen to them? When a poisonous fountain is permitted to overflow, do not its deadly waters destroy the healthy growth of all it touches?

"There is in human nature a spirit of insubordination and revolt, which, in all ages, and under

all forms of civilization, has required the necessary restraints of law ; and when a man is bold
enough in your community to defy law, it will
surely kindle a corresponding spirit in some of
his hearers.

"There is another dangerous tendency of this
fanaticism, which is too widely separating the
North and the South. While hating this institution, you look upon all the acts of Southern
men as unprincipled and corrupt, and are foster-
ing an animosity which will, in the end, lead to
bitter results.

"Look at the consequences of what has already
been done. Had it not been for the interference
of abolitionists, slavery would have been abolished
in Missouri long ago ; and this is also true of
Kentucky."

Reared under the influence of the institutions
of New England, Mr. Boomer felt their great contrast to those of his adopted State. He saw the
importance of a more general, complete, and expansive education among the people ; he felt a
great anxiety that the masses should be interested
in what would improve their own condition ; that
a more general intelligence should be diffused ;
and that he had a willing heart, as well as a

ready hand, to aid in this work, one cannot fail
to see by such resolutions as follow : —

"In the great world of city life, where all the
habits and customs have acquired the strength
of many generations, one loses his identity. If
there are evils in such a city which threaten the
good of the people and the prosperity of the
whole State, what can one puny hand do, even
though it be uplifted against them ? How can
one feeble voice be heard ?

"Brought up in the strictest sense a Puritan,
with no love for extreme views, I feel in sympathy, on some points, with both the North and
South on the subject of slavery, — an evil which
I mourn over and lament, and feel within my soul
the impulses of a man to try to eradicate, but I
am powerless. No, I am not powerless. I will
and can do something. Shame on the spirit of
man so weak that it must sit silently bowed down
to popular error and public opinion, which too
often seem to be the main principles of the world,
the mainspring of action.

"Where are the people who take the trouble to
think, or who have the moral courage to act?
Whose is the practical belief in a religion which
leads one to walk by faith and not by sight?

Where are our heroes of morality, philanthropy,
and religion? It is refreshing to read of them
in such characters as the noble Prince of Orange
or the unfaltering Martin Luther, ' who durst do
all that may become a man.'

"This is a digression. I have no expectation
of walking in the shoes even — would I might
walk in the shade — of such undying men: but
I can afar off copy their example, and try at least
to win my own self-respect by filling creditably
my little niche in life. Human nature is human
nature the world over, and it will not bear out-
rage; therefore it will not answer, at least in my
adopted State, to call men who hold slaves barbarous villains. This is the great wrong on
the part of the North, and has only served, in
this State, to injure, rather than to redress, the
condition of slavery. They will not look upon
the position of these slaveholders from any
other than their own point of view. To remove
this evil by legislation would require coercive,
violent means; but if it is to be done by social
amelioration, great kindness and consideration
must be used.

"This institution is greatly deplored in Missouri,
both for the master and slave; but the question
is, how to get rid of it, rooted and embedded as

7

it is into its most important institutions. The
master is dependent upon the slave, and in nine
cases out of ten the slave is dependent upon the
master.

. " Now it seems to me that some of the good
seed which is early sown in the minds of New-
England boys — that they have to carve their
own way in the world; that, to be men, they must
be independent ; that to cling to the uncertain fortunes of their families would beggar their existence ; that they should glory in owing to their
own merit their success in life — will do something. Here is my opportunity.

" I will build a real New-England town at Castle
Rock, and infuse into it so much of the go-ahead
element as these slow, unprogressive people can
bear. I will establish manufactories, and give to
bond and free the dignity, the stimulus, of laboring for themselves. I will build a church there.
It shall be a free Protestant church, untrammelled
by any of the follies and dogmas of the Catholic
faith. Connected with this church there must be
a Sabbath school ; and last, but not least, there
must be the common village school, ' the proudest
boast of a free people.'

" Here is a place, the school, where the rich
and the poor, the high and the low, meet upon an

equality; where the minds of all are fed alike, as the Spartans served their food upon the public table. Slavery could not live with such a state of things for many years; and I will try, in my feeble way, to help plant this undermining principle in the morning of my life, and cultivate it as I pass along, believing that in later years it will prosper."

The following notice will show the result of two years' industry : —

" The new town of Castle Rock is situated in an eminently healthy situation, at the head of the most fertile bend in the Osage River, which is navigable for steamboats to that point ten months of the year; to Linn Creek, one hundred and ten miles above, for five months in the year; and to Osceola, three hundred miles above, two and a half months in the year.

" The valley of this river contains the finest body of timber west of the Mississippi, and from it must be obtained the only permanent supply of oak timber for the construction of all the steamboats that ply the western waters above St. Louis. The quality of the lands lying on the river, especially the upper part, is well known to be unequalled for fertility in the valley of the Mississippi. Five steamboats are owned and run regularly on the river, besides many others which, during the season of high water, find profitable employment from the present large and rapidly increasing trade.

" Castle Rock is, by water, fifteen miles from the mouth of the river; by land, twelve; and from Jefferson City, the capital of the State, seven and a half miles.

" The town was laid out two years ago, by private interest, and it already contains a large and fine hotel, store, warehouses, church, blacksmith shops, wagon shops, and a number of private dwellings. Here is also one of the largest steam powers in the State, which drives a large flouring-mill and a double saw-mill of immense capacity; and there still remains a large surplus of power which can be furnished to various kinds of manufactures at a nominal price.

" Steamboat building is carried on here to a limited extent; four hulls have already been constructed."

The following testimony, to a sister of Mr. Boomer, from one of his friends in Castle Rock, gives ample proof that his ambition was not an ideal one: —

"CASTLE ROCK, July 28, 1863.

" MRS. S———.

" DEAR MADAM : Our first acquaintance with your brother began in the year 1855, about one year after he laid out the town of Castle Rock.

"At that time his steam saw-mill was in active operation, going night and day, turning out vast quantities of lumber, with which he was building steamboats, bridges, and several houses; and he also shipped large quantities to St. Louis.

"He employed a great many men, and, for so young a man, showed remarkable energy and judgment, such as would have become much older heads.

"Mr. Boomer was a great favorite, and when he visited us from St. Louis he was warmly welcomed by all, — so many crowding to see him that it would always be late before he could retire. He also loved to come among us ; and so great was his perseverance, that, in failing to get a conveyance at the mouth of the river, he has walked the whole distance, fifteen miles, after nightfall ; yet, however fatigued or immersed in business, the humblest always received a friendly recognition or warm grasp of the hand, showing that, in visiting us, he felt an interest in all.

"He was ever ready to lend a helping hand to any object of benevolence, and in cases of destitu-

7*

tion it was not enough for him to be told of it and give aid, but he must go himself, and with the donation show his sympathy, in such a kind manner as to greatly enhance the value of the gift.

"Soon after the settlement of Castle Rock, he proposed to the people that he would give the land and lumber, and build half of a church, if they would pay for the other half; but the inhabitants were slow in accepting his offer, feeling but little interest in religion. After waiting some time, seeing the general apathy on the subject, he went forward and built the church, without much assistance from those whose interest it was to have a place of worship.

"About this time the Bishop of St. Louis made him an excellent offer, in a pecuniary point of view, if he would build a Roman Catholic church, which was warmly seconded by the Germans in the vicinity; but I am truly happy to say that he did not listen to these propositions.

"His sympathies were deeply enlisted in the Sabbath school, and although crowded with business, yet he took sufficient time to visit every house in Castle Rock, inviting its inmates to come to the school.

"He took an active part in organizing the school, choosing officers, appointing teachers, and ever after, when in town, he always attended it, taking with him several persons in his employment, who would not attend at other times.

" Mr. Boomer not only gave us his presence at our school, but he also seemed to take a deep interest in the subject of the lesson, giving us his views, and making appropriate remarks. He furnished us a library of nearly three hundred volumes, with spelling books, hymn books, readers, question books, and a small map of Palestine. I mention these particulars to show his liberal spirit toward us.

. . . .

" The next year after we came here Mr. Boomer added a flour-mill to his other works, which made so fine an article as to stand with the very best flour in the St. Louis market.

" At this time Castle Rock was in a thriving condition. Houses were being built; the town was laid out into lots, and many who had bought them commenced building. Mr. Boomer had also erected a large cabinet factory, and nearly all branches of business were represented here."

In a letter to his mother, Mr. Boomer relates a touching incident in the early history of his new town : —

"Castle Rock, October 21, 1855.

"Dear Mother: I was glad to receive your letter, and hear that you was well.

"I should like to be at home this very day as much as you would like to have me there, and sit down to a good talk all quietly by ourselves; but it is not so to be. We are a long way apart, and there is a wide difference in our circumstances. You are quiet in your peaceful home; I am here quiet in my (home I cannot say) house, unfinished, sitting by the fire, in a large, dirty room, with a wash-stand for a writing-table, and a candle standing in each corner of it. This is the new hotel which we have just completed, although it is not opened really, because unfurnished.

"It is, or has been, a cold, damp day. I came out here from Jefferson City, as I have to be here to-morrow, and could not come yesterday for the rain.

"I felt rather sadly as I reached here. Our head sawyer's child was to be buried. This is the first death we have had in the place. Rather a dreary funeral.

"Mr. J—— and K—— (my agents here) had selected, this morning, the spot for the village graveyard, — a beautiful spot, too, — and all the inhabitants of our little place in the woods were at the house, ready for the funeral, — a few on horseback, but mostly on foot.

"It was too wet for the ladies to walk, so we put them in a large wagon, and started for the first grave.

"It seemed so lonely, — the little grave, — and we had no clergyman to say a service or break the seeming solitude. If I only could have obtained a Prayer Book I would have read one myself.

"Well, we came home: and as I sit before the fire, slipped down into my chair, with my feet resting upon the fireplace, looking steadily into the fire, I think of home, and when I was a boy, and the little grave, and other graves.

"Then my business comes into my head, and troubles me a little; and Mr. J—— occasionally says, 'Mr. Boomer, what do you think we had better do about so and so? Shall we not do this and get that?' I say yes, and still look at the fire, and think of everything I ever thought, I believe. And now to-morrow I shall, after dinner, go over to the railroad, where I am having the most trouble, and stay until next Saturday night, when I suppose I shall come back here again. Rather a slave's life this, and of a troublesome sort; although we all imagine that something different from what we have is desirable.

"But when I think of it, I am very happy, and have the greatest reason to be thankful. Almost everybody in the country is sick with fever, — more than half our men, — and I am remarkably well, — better than I have been for a year. We have had pleasant weather — good roads. I have a fine horse to ride, and the prospect that I shall before long be through with my business troubles.

"Give my love to father; ask him to write me. Love to all my friends.

"I am your affectionate son,

"GEORGE."

In a letter to his sister, Mr. Boomer writes: —

"I take much comfort when at Castle Rock, my Osage place, as I always delight in the idea of being in a little world of my own, and seeing it improve and grow up with myself. The thought is pleasant that, as we live along, we are doing something which is not to perish or change as the moment passes by, but which will live, not only with us, but after us."

To his mother, under date of July 10, 1856, he writes : —

" I have been at Castle Rock for nearly three weeks, and enjoyed real pleasure there.

" Three weeks to-day we inaugurated our Sabbath school, of which I took the charge on that day, and saw that it was well organized.

" The villagers have all taken a great interest in it, and I believe it will result in much good to every one.

" We had from fifty to seventy-five scholars, the majority of them Bible scholars.

" Mr. P—— and myself presented them a fine library of three hundred and fifty volumes, and an excellent melodeon, so that they have everything a school ought to have.

" We have also secured preaching every other Sabbath; we have opened a singing school, and there is a universal interest in all these things by the residents of my dear Castle Rock; and I assure you, my dear mother, if I ever enjoyed anything in life it was in being there, giving my personal assistance to these things, of such vital importance to us all."

The following extracts are from his journal: —

" September 5, 1856.

" Have made a pleasant trip to Castle Rock.
The day was beautiful, and the Osage lay placidly
among its shaded banks, as a cloud lies lazily float-
ing in the midsummer sun.

" We had a lunch after our arrival, when I sent
General G—— back in a skiff.

" The auction sale of lots commenced about
half-past one o'clock. We walked about in the
hot sun, till, coming into the shade of the wood,
the prices rose.

" I have made good sales, have inspected the
church, laid plans for new streets, and have rested
myself. I needed that.

" Went to Sabbath school, which lasted for two
hours, and I then sang a long time at Mrs. P——'s.
I love those good, sacred hymns, and feel better
for singing them. They make the heart softer
and the life purer."

" May 12, 1857.

" Dear Castle Rock! I am here in this peaceful
atmosphere again, and am somewhat at a loss to
know why I love this place so much. It is plain
to see why I should have a pride in it, why I
should be ambitious for it. That is my selfishness. But I love this place from the best of

feelings; my heart yearns over it, and the kind-hearted people who have a home here.

"Perhaps this is all indulgence of my vanity again, as, of course, this is my own realm; but I will not doubt my honesty of purpose for this place, for I believe it is a field for usefulness, which I shall be blest in filling to the best of my ability."

CHAPTER VI.

IN the mean time, while Mr. Boomer was engaged in building up his new enterprise at Castle Rock, he was not forgetful of his duties as a citizen of St. Louis. Late in the autumn of the same year that he laid the foundation of his country town, he thus writes his mother: —

"I have taken quite an interest in the new Baptist church which is trying to erect a place of worship. They have a fine lot, which was in part donated to them, and they are now erecting a chapel in the rear of it, which will cost them one thousand dollars. I gave them one hundred and fifty dollars, and promised to raise them one hundred more, making one-fourth of the expenses. If they are prospered and it is justifiable, they will build their church in the spring, which the Second Church will assist them to do, and I have promised them five hundred dollars.

"I have been unable, however, to attend many of their meetings, having been in town only two Sabbaths. They are a small body, numbering about eighty members; are not wealthy, but are strongly united. Their minister is not a man of the first order of talents, but he is a worthy man and a sensible preacher, so that I am well enough contented.

"This is in future to be my regular place of worship, because I shall feel more interest than in the old church, where I could do comparatively little good."

About the same time he wrote his father, showing not only the interest he felt in sustaining the preached gospel, but his personal need of the same.

"BUFFALO, December 12, 1854.

"DEAR FATHER: I expected to have been at home to-day, and am quite disappointed that I cannot be.

"I have been in Buffalo the last few days with Mr. S——, and am detained so long that I cannot go beyond here, as I must be in St. Louis within three or four days.

"I should so like to be at home, if only for a

short time ; for, aside from the quiet charm with which home is invested, I wanted much to have seen you and mother; to have sat down in the twilight and talked as we used to do, — talked as happy families and friends are wont in that holiest and happiest spot on the wide world's bosom — ' home ! '

"As I am more and more entangled in the tumult and strife of life, — for, though young, I have many cares, — a hurried scene appears of expectations realized and disappointed, surprises pleasurable and sad, excited pleasure, with an occasional hour of quiet happiness. I do not forget that the past is past; that the present is fast hurrying where memory will soon recall *it* as past ; that the longest future must soon be numbered with the rest ; and I solemnly resolve that my life shall not be a mere ephemeral existence, — a bark, without oars or sails or helm, borne misguidedly down the stream of time.

"Yet I am at times painfully — though not enough so — reminded that the great current bears me on, almost as purposeless as the ship without a guide, — as one who knows not where he'll end; although there are times when I hope for the better. I believe I have some purposes which are not unworthy of a man, and am conscious that in carrying out these purposes my heart must be imbued with love to God."

The winter of 1854 was one of great anxiety in the business community, and the waves of difficulty at one time seemed to rise higher and higher, threatening to engulf the whole financial world. Mr. Boomer, in speaking of these troubles, says: —

"It is hard times, and the days darken with every mail and telegraph that comes to our city. Cincinnati is experiencing a general crash: all the banks in Indiana have suspended, as well as a number in Illinois; and Chicago is, I fear, being fast overtaken with the panic.

"St. Louis will, I think, without much trouble, stand the shock, as everything here is done upon a safe principle. I can only say that, so far, we are safe, and, unless it comes worse yet, we shall continue so; but it is trying times, and we shall be very fortunate if we get through without a rub."

Not only did he attend faithfully to the arduous duties of his business during that winter, but he also found time for study, which he playfully details to one of his sisters: —

8*

"At half-past twelve o'clock I ordinarily take dinner at Mons. Boileau's, my French teacher's. We have soup—excellent; sometimes roast beef; sometimes boiled meat; bread, without butter; apples, but no pastry. Well, you see, if I don't like it, it is a sacrifice to obtain literature, and so I am a martyr. I take tea at the same place; after which comes my French lesson."

In the summer of 1855 Mr. Boomer had a severe illness; and although most kindly cared for by friends, yet he felt keenly the want of a home, and decided to make himself more comfortable in that respect. His new arrangements he describes in the following letter: —

"St. Louis, June 12, 1855.

"My dear Sister: I suppose you have learned the particulars of my illness through mother; therefore I will not burden you with a second edition of its details. I was confined to my bed three weeks, but by no means alone or uncared for. My good friends, Mr. and Mrs. McP———, took me to their delightful, hospitable home, and treated me with the greatest kindness; in fact, I had the best of care and nursing. So you see that I have not suffered for anything. There are ministering angels always hovering about our earth.

"I intend to take the best care of myself possible; and, in order to be quiet and comfortable, have gone to keeping 'bachelor's hall.' What think you? That I am very unwise, I presume.

"Well, perhaps so; nevertheless, I am going to try it. I have a small house, situated upon a very pleasant street, with good shade and breeze. The contents thereof, in rooms, are, a parlor, dining-room, and kitchen below, and the same number of rooms up-stairs.

"Our draftsman lives with me, and is regularly installed as steward; for cook and maid-of-all-work I have a faithful colored woman. I assure you her kitchen answers to 'the white-washed wall and nicely sanded floor' which Goldsmith found so many years ago.

"So far, housekeeping is a great success. It is much better for my health, as I can command wholesome food am more quiet, and can regulate much better my hours for sleep. If some gentle 'Portia' would now appear, who would love me as 'Brutus's wife' loved her husband, — oh, what a lucky fellow! But I am content for the present."

After being fully settled in his new home, he had an opportunity of testing its comforts and expediency, as he was prostrated by another illness. On recovering, he wrote his parents : —

"I assure you I have thought of you often, and for the first time, when sick, was a little out of heart one day. Any of your dear faces would have been very welcome. Yet, when I think how well I am situated, how comfortably settled in my little home, with plenty of kind friends who call and see me as often as I could wish, with everything, in fact. that head or heart could desire, I feel ashamed to be otherwise than cheerful and happy. I reflect, too, how easily everything might have been far otherwise and worse for us all; and I try to be thankful to Him who gives us all things, that he has disposed of our interests as he has. I know I do not feel thankful enough, and pray that I may in future; although when we are well, and gliding along in the boat of life, it is difficult to hear anything but the dipping of the oars and the murmur of the stream.

"I am really much better, and am improving fast. I beg you will not let this illness of mine trouble you, though, of course, I should feel badly did you not have some solicitude on my account. Still, it will do no good to let it make you unhappy, and the thought that it did so would give me additional pain."

A letter to one of his sisters, of a few weeks' later date, gives ample proof that Mr. Boomer's heart did not grow less tender towards his early home, notwithstanding his wide separation from it, the engrossing cares of an extensive business, and the flatteries which the world pays to one who has been uncommonly successful.

"St. Louis, December 29, 1855.

"DEAR SISTER: I have just read over again your letter, which was received long ago. It is a dear good letter, and I feel better for reading it, for it brings to me pleasant recollections and peaceful thoughts, which are happy interludes in my half-stormy, half-vexatious life.

"You speak of the cold weather, the piles of snow, of the children skating on the orchard pond, and of Johnny looking like me as a boy; all makes me think of my boyhood, or, rather, long for it; and then I think I never had a boyhood proper, for from a child I was thrown into the position of a man, and I begin to feel it now. I fear I have had too much care for my years.

"As I read your letter, I picture to myself a scene, a life, such as I have often imagined would have been for us all the perfection of happiness, that is, so far as it would depend upon outward circumstances. The basis of it is a home. I sigh for the recollection of such a home, — one old, grown gray, and tottering with the passing years; or a wide-spread farm, with clear brooks, gray hills, green valleys, dark and deep old woods, shadowed over with ancient trees, with ivy climbing round, fresh and green, as though gladdening with the thought that time was fast making mouldy walls to give him a hale old age; — with orchards, too, ponds and meadows, a mossy old well-curb, and, to complete the scene (no imagination), —

'With all the loved spots
That my infancy knew.'

"As I sit in my arm-chair, gazing at nonentity, heedless of the tread and noise of thousands passing by, I wish it had been so, and that we were all children yet and at home, — innocent, careless, and happy in the joys of our childhood life.

"But I sigh again, and say, although we never had so picturesque a home, yet it was true and loving; and here we are, thousands of miles apart, each fighting for himself or herself a way through this chilly, stormy world. Then I stare at nothing, look blue a while longer, take a long breath, and say, 'Oh, well. It is well enough; best, perhaps, as it is,' — and philosophically drum on the piano.

"We have had, for us, a severe winter, a great deal of snow. Yesterday, last night, and a part of to-day, it has been snowing incessantly, and it still comes down to remind me of what a New-England snow-storm is; yes; more than that, — of a home, and those dear friends there!

"I wonder if it snows about your house to-day. I should like to see it, for this snow puts me in a kind of passion. It comes down steadily and sternly as though it intended to cover up all the old-fashioned farm-houses, and only leave little holes at the chimneys for the smoke to get out at, and snow porches at the doors for the people to creep out at, when the storm is over. It comes as though it was going to enlarge all the gates, walls, and fences, whiten all the trees, and keep the stock in the barn.

"And then, when the snowing is all over, with you come the beauties and sports of winter; but with us the scene of pure, white snow is spoiled

by one day of bright sunshine, and changed to
mud and dirt."

Mr. Boomer felt a great interest in Missouri
from the earliest history of Castle Rock. He saw
the necessity of labor in the country, and offered
every inducement in his power to persons of
intelligence and enterprise to settle there. He
built houses of comfort and convenience, and finished them with as much taste as was practicable,
so that a home could be provided at once to new
settlers. He cultivated an acquaintance with the
people of the country around, — those who had
been proprietors of the soil for many years, particularly, — and showed them, in every way, that
he wished to promote their interests. When he
could command a day from his many arduous
duties it would frequently be spent with them;
and thus, soon after the little township began to
grow, he united with the people in the country
in celebrating our national independence, telling
them, as he said, "a few common-place things in
a common-place way:" —

"I cannot deny myself the pleasure of saying to
you a few words on this the galaday of our national freedom.

"This is the anniversary of our independence as a nation; and every pulsation of the human heart thrills at the return of this birthday of our liberty; a day such as has never gilded the brightest page of any nation's history before.

"What a joy and pride, then, for us, in the quiet and retirement of our country homes, — surrounded by all this beauty and wealth of God's munificent creation, so rich and full and overflowing in blessings to us as a people, — to commemorate that peculiarly glorious independence which we often complacently say is the purest man has ever possessed.

"Let us eulogize it, then, and commemorate its individual character, — make national character and national independence essential, yes, vital to the dignity of our country, — remembering, first of all, that in communities independence should be exercised with due reference to the equal privilege of all to enjoy the same high prerogative.

"We, who now behold the sun of liberty in its mid-day splendor, are too apt, like the sluggard rising at noon, to forget the struggles of early morning; our vision, under the influence of its effulgent rays, is narrowed to the present moment.

"On that memorable morning, July 4th, 1776,

9

our forefathers, as they arose and looked upward, saw no sun in mid-heaven to lull them into apathy. The dawn was only breaking. It was not an unclouded morn, and the eastern breezes brought from across the wide waters the sound of clanking chains. It was a knell of early days, and roused them to heroic action.

"But we may go still further back, before the darkness of that long night of the middle ages had been penetrated by the sun of the 'New World,' when the east winds swept over Europe only to drive our forefathers from their native lands and cherished homes across a pathless ocean, gladly braving its dangers and its perils, to a dreary, unknown wilderness. And for what? Ah, yes, fellow-citizens, for what? To secure our liberty, and, through us, liberty to our posterity. How could human action be more grand than this? I cannot conceive in this world a sight more sublime than that of our noble forefathers, as they landed at Jamestown and Plymouth, stepping out boldly upon our inhospitable shores; some of them to live by long and hard toil and struggle, but most of them to die; to die away from all those associations they loved and cherished, with the memories of youth and childhood clinging around them; to die in a cold and comfortless land, amidst the wild forests, while the yell of savages waited to sound their requiem, and the winds of our stormy Atlantic howled along the rocky shore ; to die calmly and fearlessly, trusting in God, strong in a sublime faith that they had sown the seed which would, in after years, bear imperishable fruit, — seed which would outlive all the storms and frosts of that fearful time.

"The noble example of our forefathers took firm root in the hearts of their children : so firm, that neither storms, frosts nor chains could eradicate it. Through all the tempests of those perilous years it lived, when men at once fought and prayed and toiled for daily bread ; when burning homes and desolated fields only kindled higher and higher the flames of liberty, and the blood that flowed as water from the sides of massacred wives and children only swelled broader and deeper the stream of freedom, until it deluged and swept the land, — until liberty became a birthright, a household god, which came with life. and went only with death !

"It was these sacrifices, to which they had been inured from childhood, that enabled our forefathers, a feeble but united band, to defy, in their wild and scattered homes, the power of one-

half the world. 'We are three millions of free-
men,' said they; 'let us die in defence of our
liberties!' That noble sentiment withstood and
aroused the world, and the wondering nations
stood aloof to behold the sight, until, one by one,
they came to a tardy recognition of our rights.

   .   .   .   .

"The strength of our early fathers lay in their
virtue, in their consciousness of right; a power
which enables man to stand up alone, if need be,
against the world; to die any death calmly and
happily for the cause he has espoused.

   .   .   .   .

"If such are the principles of liberty and self-
government which our Puritan fathers planted
and nurtured for us amid such peril, how tenderly
should we cherish them; and if it required such
sacrifices to bring forth the plant in its tender
years, we should take care lest weeds and thorns
grow up around it now, and mar its beauty of
riper age. Rome was strong in her youth; but
when the once barren soil had grown rich with
the cultivation and wealth of years, the weeds of
corruption grew up around her, and choked out
her strength and life."

Mr. Boomer spent quite a portion of the years

1856 and 1857 in different parts of the State. This was a consequent necessity of his business ; but he also found it interesting and profitable to familiarize himself with the present condition and future prospects of Missouri.

That the development of all new States must have for its foundation agriculture, was doubtless one of the principles which governed him in his Castle Rock enterprise. It seemed an easy thing to him for any man of industrious habits, surrounded by such regions of fertile soil, abundantly watered, and in so fine a climate, to become of real importance to the wealth of Missouri as a farmer; therefore he gave to that department of labor his personal encouragement by clearing a township of land.

But notwithstanding the value of the farmer and the merchant, the men most needed, in his opinion, in building up the State into a structure of real beauty, were mechanics. He says that recent investigations have shown that the richness of this State in iron ore is incalculable ; and the people of Missouri should be earnest in turning this vast resource to their immediate and perpetual prosperity. They should, without delay, offer every inducement to manufacturers to

9

convert it into use, — which will tend greatly to
complete the material civilization of the State.

He also became interested in the lead mines,
and the firm made an extensive purchase of three
thousand acres of pine and mineral land in Washington County. This property was located in the
town of Potosi, on a branch of the Iron Mountain
Railroad, sixty-five miles from St. Louis.

These lands were selected with great care, on
account of their heavy growth of timber, and
from the fact that there were no pine forests in
the western part of the State, or in Kansas or
Nebraska. The market for this lumber would not
only be good in St. Louis, but large quantities
must be annually sent up the Missouri River.
This property was also the centre of the great
lead fields of Missouri. The mineral wealth was
valuable, and several exceedingly rich mines had
been discovered.

As a natural result of this enterprise, a little
settlement sprung up, comprising a large saw-
mill, with circular saws, edging and lath saws, a
shingle machine, and a blacksmith's shop. These
workshops necessitated dwelling-houses, a store,
etc.

This additional field of industry gave him not
only a wider range throughout the State, but it

imposed upon him corresponding obligations connected with its inhabitants, — obligations which
he did not tire of performing, when by so doing
he could gratify or benefit them.

He was invited to address the citizens of West-
phalia on the 4th of July, 1857. Some extracts
from his remarks on that occasion are here introduced : —

"It is reasonable and wise that we, as citizens
of a great, progressive, and free nation, should,
during one day in the year, repose from our
various labors, and assemble to thank the great
Giver of all blessings for the continuance, thus
far, of those mercies which he gave our forefathers strength to win for us, and to ask of him,
in a becoming manner, their perpetuity unto our
posterity.

"It is reasonable and wise that, on such a day
as this, the stillness of the land should testify
to that peaceful prosperity which the industrial
promptings of social equality have brought us ;
that the sound of the mills should cease ; that
the fabric of the factory should stand in the
loom or the lathe ; that the hammer should rest
on the forge ; that commerce should repose at the
wharves ; that the harvest should await the hus-

bandman; and that old men and matrons, young
men and maidens, childhood and youth, should
come together, bid industry adieu awhile, send
memory back to the past with its pleasant face,
and turn towards hope, which holds up the future
with a smile.

"The youth, when walking the road up those
mountains on whose heights history has builded
her temple, reposes by the wayside in the heat
of the summer's day, and refreshed by the hour,
cheered by the journey past, is stimulated for the
ascent beyond. So then, to-day, in the heat of
the summer's sun, we rest an hour by the wayside, while walking steadily the road of progress
up those heights where we hope to finish a structure, already begun, better than this proud world
has ever reared before; and, cheered by the past,
we shall gather strength by the hour to work on
the way beyond.

"If we may justly claim to be free, great, and
prosperous as a nation, the causes that have
worked out for us such a position are worthy
our frequent and earnest study. If we are basking in the splendor of a government better than
the world has ever known, a fact so marked in
history must be underlaid by causes which that
history has not yet unfolded concerning those

states which have already risen, flourished, and
passed away. Yet the truths of that record have
their negative importance, to teach the legitimate
effect of the causes producing them. So, by
analysis, when we discover those various causes
working out, with the certainty of universal law,
sooner or later, their legitimate end in the sure
destruction of each state or organized society in
which their operations can be traced, we may
hope for a happier result; a result which will
teach us not to miss the better law, developing
its inherent principle in a beneficent, and, we
may hope, an enduring prosperity. Thus, learning error, we may discover truth.

"The one great deception, which the world
has perniciously clung to, has been reliance upon
physical, material power. 'Might makes right'
has been the world's practical philosophy, religion,
and morality, from the age of the Pharaohs until
now, so that each growing age pulls down the
weaker one passing away.

.   .   .   .

"Great, progressive, and free! Potent words,
pregnant with thought, action, and principle:
pregnant with power, progress, and perfection;
pregnant with the greatest finite result of humanity — civilization.

"There is a question pendent here which the world is solving, which we are solving, which posterity is yet to solve ; a question fraught with interest to humanity ; a question vital to its finite perfection ; and that question is, the extent of the human capacity ; — whether there be in man a germ of progress, which, if planted in the early gardens of the world, cultivated in the fields which civilization has prepared, will ripen into a harvest whose fruit, when the gathering time shall come, will be deemed fit to be transferred to a new earth, a better land ; whether, in fact, civilization, in its proudest and best sense, is progressive. I believe it is ; and this has induced me to say that we are a nation great, progressive, and free ; that we are bearing a part, and a great one too, in the march of progress, — pressing on to fuller developments of civilization.

"The fatality attending ancient civilization is attributable to its limited character or narrow extent. Intellectually, ancient society contained but one element, or represented but one power, which uprooted others. Not that the various elements natural to an organized society did not incipiently exist and contend for their relative positions, but one of those many assumed proportions too great for the existence of the others, and they were overshadowed, died, and left society subject to one idea, one element, one power, and that power was theocracy.

.   .   .   .

"For the development of profound thoughts and ideas in the fine arts, we are directed to ponder the 'mouldering records of ages,' and read there the perfections of those ripe years. True, the lustre of that age has remained almost undimmed by the shades and mists of many centuries; still, we may look for fairer, more harmonious proportion in the building of our glorious Republic, if, as architects, we study with becoming interest the grandeur of our work.

"This beautiful structure of ours is not entrusted to the genius of one mind, whose whole thoughts and life have been given to the investigation of real and ideal excellence, the blending of external and internal perfection. No : we each, and every one of us, as citizens of these United States, have a part to act in forming the beauty of this structure.

"Let us see to it, then, how we use the materials of our work. Let us see to it that we do not undermine the strength of our Union through selfishness, ignorance, or wilfulness, — a Union which God has given us the means of making perfect in its arrangement of mutually supporting parts, mutually related forces, all combined to attain a perfect and glorious end."

CHAPTER VII.

"St. Louis, January 8, 1858.

MY DEAR MOTHER: I have made within the last year a partnership in house-keeping, and in that way have bettered my condition, by a more commodious house, and an agreeable companion, whose tastes and mine are almost one.

"This is an economical arrangement also; and I feel it a duty not only to live within my means, but to avoid ostentation or extravagance in these times, when so many young men are ruining themselves, their families, their business, and, in some instances, their employers, by reckless expenditures, which soon lead to vices too often criminal.

"It pains me when I think of the habits of our young men. Many of them, who receive limited salaries, or at best but a small income from their business, rush into methods of spending time, into scenes of amusement, where they can throw away the most money, thereby acquiring the reputation

10

of being 'up to the times' and 'the prince of good
fellows.' We have had many instances throughout our country lately, showing too plainly that,
by thus living beyond one's honest income, and
that, too, without any high moral or social aims,
many young men have indulged in highly criminal
practices to support their assumed artificial positions.

"Fast living, 'Young Americanism,' and extravagance in every form, is the peculiar evil of
our time. It degrades the moral character, cor-
rupts the mind, and vitiates the taste. It is eat-
ing into the very vitals of all that is sound and
vigorous in our religious, moral, social, and political society; and unless our young men who have
worth, honor, and aims worthy their positions, will
see this evil and reform it, I can but see in the
future a corrupt and dissolute picture, — a picture
more distorted than the good men of our country
would have dared to fear for their sons when they
left them a land blessed and enlightened by a
Christianity of primitive simplicity and a system
of universal education. I have been alarmed on
this subject recently from the fact that an increasing number of young men have been convicted as
defaulters; and I have realized more fully than

ever the force of that homely maxim, that 'an honest name is better than great riches.'"

One of the most noble traits of Mr. Boomer's character was his strong, earnest, and unchanging affection for his own family ; and although removed from them in early life, both by distance and circumstances, yet the bond which linked his soul to theirs was like the warp and woof, woven fast. His elder sister had been greatly afflicted in the loss of several of her children. This was a deep sorrow to his sympathetic heart. He mourned his inadequacy to console her, his unworthiness in the presence of so great an affliction. Still, under date of March 28, 1858, he writes : —

"MY DEAR SISTER: I cannot refrain from writing you a short letter, not only in answer to yours, but from what I learned through Cousin C——B——, who has just come from Worcester. — that your youngest child is dead.

"My dear sister, what can I say to you? How shall I offer you the sympathy of a brother? I do not know. Your afflictions have been so frequent, so severe, and so unlooked for, that I, so far away, can feebly realize them in the bitterness of their severity, and can poorly offer you those heart-rending, gushing feelings of pity and sorrow which I know I should feel were I with you, and which the greatness of your suffering and the poignancy of your grief require from those who love you. But such as it is, take it; take it always; and ever be sure, when well or ill, when happy or weighed down with misfortunes, that you have the love, the sympathetic heart, poor as it is, of your brother George.

"I cannot attempt to console you; I feel myself unworthy. I know too well I could not console myself under such circumstances, and it would be sacrilege for me to offer you a consolation I can lay no claim to myself. You have a resource far above mine, that never fails, even when misery lays its heavy hand upon you, and you will seek it now; and when you do, remember, amid all the rest, a bad but good-hearted brother far away.

"I will write no more, save to ask Mr. D——— to accept my well-wishes and my kindest sympathy.

"I will send a great deal of love to Amelia, and Johnny especially. Tell him his uncle bids him be ambitious to be good, and he will be far happier for it when a man.

"I am alone in my parlor, except Cousin C——, who wishes to be kindly remembered.

"I think of you and feel sadly, and as I retire to rest I will, in an unworthy way, ask God to bless you, and remember you kindly in your latter years."

To the same person, April 10 : —

"Your sweet letter came to me in due time, and gave me pleasure, though a sad one : but sometimes I love a sad pleasure most. There is a tinge of melancholy in my nature that floats about my thoughts, in a dreamy way, so often, and with such constancy, that I love it, and when it goes away I sometimes wish it back again, for, as it softens down the brightness of exuberant joy, so it lightens up the gloom of a dark and poignant grief.

"As I read your letter I thought how sadly, yet how sweetly, you bear the heavy load which misfortune lays upon you ; and looking away into the dim future, I could almost see you looking there too, thinking that when time lifts its curtain, at the end of life, you could again behold your children, — gone from you now, — where, folded

10*

in your arms, they would call you mother once
more, in that future, blessed land. I do not wonder that, with such hopes, with such thoughts,
you can submit to your fate resignedly, and bear
your sorrows calmly, though they come sudden
and fast.

   .   .   .   .

  " Though it is at once a sorrow and a pleasure
to think of the past, — of those hours which were
happier than now, — yet it is a duty to make the
present in some degree as cheerful to ourselves
and others as the times which were ; for they are
gone, and we are not made to ruminate entirely
over what we can no longer control, but to improve what we have. I have thought often of
you, and of those who were but are not now, and
have tried to sympathize with you ; but, alas ! I
am so poorly fitted to do so. I wish it were otherwise, — that I were a better man ; but the cares
and busy affairs of life are a loadstone, and draw
man's heart along piece by piece, until all is
there."

  To another sister, who was passing through the
trial of giving up a dear home, he extends his
sympathy as follows : —

"St. Louis, April 15, 1858.

"Dear S——: I am always glad to get a letter from you, but your last made me a little sad.

"I know you better than most people do, and can understand without your telling me that the sundering of the ties of your dear home would be a great trial. It would be to me, my dear, noble-hearted sister; and I am sorry for you, for I love you.

"I will make you a visit certainly very soon, and we will talk over old times, and present times, and times to come. We will be happy a little while, anyhow, and we will try to be so all the time; and if we try hard, we shall, because our happiness is more within than without us, and nothing can take it away. So we will not stifle and crush it, but love and cherish it; and when misfortune or age creep on, it will love and cherish us, and lead us, blind though we may be, along a peaceful way, that will open and end on the shores of eternal rest.

"I am a little sentimental, my sister, but I can't help it; for if what I say comes from my heart,— and I am sure it does,— it had better be out than in; for if it dies there and rots, bad matter will come of it, which will grow dark, rank weeds, that will poison the air there, and then my heart will

die; and it is better to have a foolish heart than
no heart. I know it will make no difference to
you what kind of a letter I write; you will love
me just the same; and so I feel safe in scribbling
on at random just as I feel.

"Now as to your letter. You must not be sick,
and you must not be low-spirited. You must
make everybody love you, because you must love
everybody, and you must make everybody happy,
because you are happy all the time. So, when
you go to your new home, you must make everybody there happy, and then you will be happy,
too, — won't you?

"Don't you see how much you can do? It is
a pretty place where you are going, and you can
have a nice home, a good horse and carriage, and
take long drives along the lake. I will be there,
too, sometimes, when we will drive together to see
the sun set in summer nights, when day bids the
world good-by, and twilight stands over the lake
to bless its going and welcome its successor.
Your husband will be prosperous in his business
there, your little girls will be with you, our dear
home will be nearer, and all will be well if you
make it well, and ill if you make it so.

"I am not afraid of the result of this change to
you, although sorry for your present disappoint-

ment. There is a certain charm to me in seeing those I love pass through the necessary discipline of life as becomes true men and women. We cannot tell what true metal is until it has passed through the refining process."

The following extracts are from his journal: —

"May 2, 1858.

"I here open this new book, where I will record the impressions of the days as they pass. These thoughts I will commit to the sleepy genius of my pen, which must come forth every night from his dark hole in my drawer, and rub, rub along, marking my dull thoughts on the nice white sheets of my '*au fait*' little book. Poor, sleepy pen, — I will not keep him up long, but put him back in his hole, close the book, shut up the thoughts, close the dark drawer on them both, and lock the pen, thoughts, and the darkness in; then drowsily go up the stairs and close the sheets on myself, my thoughts, and the darkness, till daylight turns the key and the morn breaks in.

"But the key will turn hard with us, — for we are sleepy things, — the pen and me, and our thoughts. I certainly am so now, and the ideas do not flow half so brilliantly as they did during the

day, when the reading of ' *Les Confidences* ' made
the idea almost a new one,—what a happy thing,
years hence, ever so badly written a journal of
events and impressions would be, — or as they did
an hour past when I was writing to my sisters;
for since then I have been interrupted by a long
conversation with Mr. H——.

"I have just laid down 'Chapin's City Life,' to
write my first memoranda in this new book.   I
fear I shall often fail in making daily work of it,
but will hope for the best, as I am satisfied that if
I write but little, that little can do no harm.

"It has been a rainy, gloomy day; and, what
is unusual for me, I have been in-doors most
of the time, settling up some private accounts
for the last month; after which I indulged myself
in reading ' *Les Confidences* ' until dinner, which
was fine enough for ten men instead of two.

"After dinner W—— started out in the rain,
but came back, remarking that the umbrella looked
fine and was ornamental, but that a porous state of
affairs rendered it unpleasant in the open air.

"Toward evening I made some calls on my
friends, taking tea with one of them, and coming
home before nine o'clock.   I was reading my
Bible, when Mr. D—— came in, as he alleged, in
pursuit of Mr. H——.   Soon after his leaving,

I fell to writing my letters, as I have already
asserted. I am now going to bed. I hear it rain-
ing outside, and it feels more cheerful within.
I will make a feeble, and I fear but half-earnest,
prayer, and sleep on till to-morrow."

" May 3.

"After tea, W—— and myself were enjoying
a quiet time together, reading and talking, when
some of our friends came in and insisted upon our
going with them to Mr. B——'s, to go through
the ceremony previous to Miss B——'s marriage
to-morrow night. We went, and had a pleasant
evening.

' How silvery sweet sound lovers' tongues by night !'

It is now eleven o'clock as I sit here with my
pencil, previous to going to bed, after having
read a little from 'Prescott's Conquest of Peru.' "

" May 4.

" I have just come home from the wedding,
— four o'clock. What unpardonable dissipation !
But it is the beautiful spring ' of hope, and love,
and youth, wind-winged emblem.' Well, now
let me write down some of the incidents of the
evening, which has stretched itself far through
the night. We had supper early. After tea I

took an elegant French lesson, and read long
pages from M——, the most beautiful and ex-
quisite thing, so far, that I have read in French.
I was charmed with the book; so much so, that I
was happy with myself for the first time in a
month. I dressed for the wedding, and hurried
that I might witness the ceremony. I found I
was too early, so came home and sat down, reading a while, and went back too late. W—— and
myself made our debut together. It has been an
elegant affair. I was in fine humor, danced and
talked fast with sundry people, the bride among
others, who looked beautiful, and was not dressed
excessively, but with taste. At half-past ten
o'clock I went to Miss S——'s wedding, which
was charming. The grounds were superb, con-
taining some charming people, with a charming
supper in a charming little room, which passed a
charming little place under the stairs, where cold
water stood, but where other things were swal-
lowed besides solids and liquids. J—— T——
drove me home, and as I stepped from the door
to the pavements and looked through the street
away over the river, the light was faintly but
brightly breaking upon the eastern sky. As I
wished the bride good-night, I prayed that her
nights might always close with as bright a dawn."

"St. Louis, Sunday night, May 7, 1858.

"That is a big heading. Well, we must always begin with a flourish to make an impression, and this is a journal of impressions; though many people claim that their proper home is in the heart instead of the head; mayhap, if so, they are domestic in their character, — too much so, I am half inclined to believe.

"The heart receives an impression, and, if it be kind or noble, it clings to it, feeds on it, nourishes it with its own warmth, its own love, while the brain sees the flame from afar, and puts forth to the world its counterfeit. In those moments, however, when man rises superior to his mental self, his moral, his devotional, and his sympathetic nature arouse and exhibit his divine ideal; then the heart throbs with its impressions; — impressions of the past and gone, impressions of the present great reality, impressions of the future, terrible expectancy, and the soul speaks out to tell its fellows, and to tell itself, the grandeur of its nature. What are the impressions it reveals? Can they be written? Was the highest of man's moral nature ever known to other than himself except through sympathy? If I had time I would write, but it is near twelve o'clock, and to-morrow I must be up betimes. So a little of to-day. This

11

morning I went to church, took dinner with Mr.
P——, after which we sang a little in his room.
I then came home, took my books, and read. I
feel a consciousness of hours misspent, of dissatis-
faction with myself. I wish I could make a nobler
record of my life ; but, alas ! "

" May 11.

"After settling the financial questions of the
day, I gave my attention to an engine for the new
mill at Washington County. When through that, I
came home and took my French lesson. After
supper was over, I sat down to the piano and tried
some new music which I had bought for a friend.
Then came business again. It is now late, I am
tired, and feel, as I often do, that much of my time
is spent unwisely. But what avail these regrets?
Man is not capable of controlling and sustaining
himself in any good and worthy course of life, and
must be aided by a reliance upon some higher,
purer fountain of action than that which lies
within him. One feature of our character may
bind and control all others, but, unless it be
the moral feature, it will be utterly deficient.
Self-esteem may control and perfect many of
our habits, but it will degenerate us into egotists.
Avarice may drive us from many follies, yet

it will entail to us new follies greater than
itself. Ambition may make our whole being trib-
utary to it, but what so hollow as ambition?
Ah! there is nothing gives the soul comfort
but the consciousness that its motives are pure
in the sight of God.

"I have been sitting here for an hour, reading in Cicero and a chapter from Alhambra,
and I could write a long time to-night : still,
as I must be up early in the morning to go to
Hannibal, it will not do. So good-night to my
journal. I am locking you up here, to turn
your pages over again on a rainy day, in the
long future years, should my life be spared."

On May 17th, Mr. Boomer records in his memoranda the incidents of his trip to Hannibal and
its business details, mentioning also that he had
been able to add to his little store of knowledge
of the Jews by a review of Jewish history. He
says : —

"On returning, I met on board the steamer
a Mr. L——, with whom I had a very agreeable conversation. He is a man well informed,
with clear views of principles, life, and men,
and with large and varied experience. It is

pleasant to meet a man who will sit down with you and appreciate your feelings and thoughts of the world, of men, and of life.

"I would like to know and associate more with men who think, and who know how to apply thought, and who, in gathering the materials for it, have sought what mind has always sought, — the experience of the world, — and where mind has always sought it, — from the record of that experience, condensed, analyzed, and classified by the greatest minds. I need some one my superior, one who possesses what I lack, to control, by his association and example, the actions and the habits of my life.

"I believe the professed objects of my life are right in the main; but how badly followed! Can I never be what I wish to be? Will I never have the physical and moral courage to change my present half-wasting way of spending time? When life is so real, can I not be in earnest?"

Mr. Boomer was never a member of any church, although he frequently resolved to make a public profession of religious faith. He was educated in the Baptist denomination, and all his family had been identified with that religious body; still, he did not, as mature years advanced, indorse their views of church organization, but, feeling great respect and veneration for his early education, he found it hard to break away from these influences. It is evident that he was unsettled for a time on this subject: but he remarked to a friend, not long before his death, that the reason he had not united with the Episcopal Church, before entering the field, was purely accidental. That he felt the power and necessity of Christianity as an institution, has been already seen; that he realized its importance as a personal possession, may be further seen by some self-searching reflections found in journals and letters: —

"Every man, who has the mind and the faculties of a man, is personally accountable to God for his religious belief. If this be not true, why has man reason, a conscience, a will? What are the functions of those organs? Are they independent or dependent?

"In this world man is both independent and dependent; for he is a presumer, an arrogant man, who ignores all the light which centuries of study and research have given to the world: but must he believe the faith of his fathers correct

11*

without the sanction of his own approval? Then
he denies the doctrine of free-will, and his conscience is the conscience of his ancestors. No,
this cannot be truth; for if man is denied the
rights of personal investigation, his reason is a
useless thing. This idea is contrary to the first
principles of education or the development of
the human mind.

"The voice of inspiration and reason is, that
I am to be taught, not controlled; to be in-
structed, not commanded; for every one of God's
creatures is plainly told that he must work out
his own salvation with fear and trembling, and
that he is to give an account of his own steward-
ship, whether it be good or bad."

"I have within the last few months made
some questions in theology an earnest, and, I believe, a prayerful study. I would not be deceived
on the most important of all subjects; far better
give up all other cherished hopes than to make
a sacrifice of this; for the time will come with
me, as with all men, when I must have this sure
staff to lean upon. God grant that it may not be
a broken reed.

"I have examined with care the doctrines
and the history of the powerful Church of Rome.

It is a wonderful history, and many of its magnificent appointments awe me. I have been tempted to embrace the doctrines of this church; but I cannot find in my Bible that God has any vicegerent on earth; I cannot find it in my reason or conscience; I cannot find that it would make man a purer being were such the case. God must be man's only appeal; none other can do helpless sinners good; and however the emotions of the heart may be stirred by the pomp of this imposing church, yet I believe the more simple and unpretending man is in his worship of the Deity, the more acceptable it is in the eyes of Him who knows every secret thought of the heart. From the recesses of a lowly spirit the humble prayer must ascend; and the poor publican felt no need of lofty dome or roll of anthem to bring him into the sacred presence of the great Physician of souls.

"What a beautiful lesson of humility! Ah, that is the point, — humility and submission. Man is proud and self-sufficient; he grows away from that teachable, child-like spirit required of every one who would enter into an eternal rest.

"How wonderful and sublime are the lessons of humility taught us by our Divine Lord, as we read them in his exhortations that we be

forgiving and charitable to one another! It is
not strange, when envy, malice and selfishness
are so predominant in human nature, that our
Saviour saw the importance of leaving us that
remarkable description of charity. Surely, never
man spake like that. No poet's tongue or phi-
losopher's pen could give such lessons to the world.
What tenderness and forbearance flowed from his
lips and life! And love, too, love was his con_
stant theme. What an injunction he laid upon
his disciples, as he drew near the end of his
earthly pilgrimage: 'A new commandment give I
unto you, that ye love one another.'"

"St. Louis, June 4, 1858.

"My dear Sister: It is, I think, about half-
past nine this Sunday evening. I have not been
to church to-day, but to-night I have been thinking of my home, my father, my mother, my sister,
and friends, who live away amid the surroundings and recollections of my childhood.

"I am feeling a little sadly; but it is well, for I
am led to think of that Source from which both
sadness and happiness flow. I have been reading
my Bible, and supplicating the Author of all good
that he would give me strength to withstand and
put off the temptations of my life.

"I see and feel the truth, the effect of Christianity, through almost a blindness of faith, which I cannot bring myself to confess without violence to all the truth of my nature: yet I do recognize the weakness of mortality, its degenerating tendency, and the necessity of its support from an immortal and omnipotent Power. To that Power I have often prayed, and will continue to pray that he will lead me, his erring creature, by his love, along the highway he has destined me to travel, so that my course shall not do violence to his will, or wrong to those who travel with me along the road which God, in his infinite goodness, gives us to journey through on our way to himself.

"I am constantly reminded of the inexpressible wisdom and kindness which God has manifested towards this world, and of its ingratitude in return. I do devoutly pray that he will give me the wisdom to see my own ingratitude, the penitence to atone for it, and sufficient of the spirit of his love to warm my own with devotion to him and his glory alone.

"My dear sister, I have never written to you such sentiments as these before; yet, for months past, and at times for years, I have felt myself terribly sinful, and have devoutly prayed to my

Maker that he would make me a better man. I
sometimes fear that I make little improvement;
but in striving after a purer life I find happiness."

"Oh for the rarity of Christian charity! Why
is it that when differences arise on moral questions
there is so much bitterness intermixed with it?
Men contend sharply on political questions with
perfect good-nature ; they quarrel in business
to-day and are good friends to-morrow; but when
the conscience, when duty is the umpire, how
unflinching the will becomes!

"God is love. Love is the essence of religion;
and whoever possesses it cannot long indulge in
bitterness of heart towards any of God's creatures. This is an unfailing test of personal religion : if a man hate his brother how can he love
his God?"

"ST. LOUIS, May 30.

"There is a very general interest felt now
throughout the country on the subject of religion;
it is visible here in our little Third Church, which
is full, even crowded, on the Sabbath. Meetings
are held every evening, and sixty-five have been
already added to the church. All the churches are
prospering, and business men's prayer-meetings are
held every day at twelve o'clock."

" POTOSI, June 12, 1858.

" I came here yesterday to close some sales of property we have made, and, being through with my business, am sitting about, with my book, on the porch of a country inn.

" We have been having a delightful shower, which makes the corn look as smiling as a happy maiden when she awakes from bright dreams. What a universal blessing is a shower in summer!

." Potosi is an old, dilapidated town; it had its palmy days thirty years ago. Settled largely by French, about ninety years since, its principal citizens acquired wealth and indolence from the immense lead business done here at that time; but when the crash of 1837 came, labor went away, and nothing has remained except the proprietors, who live on what former days did for them, and who, wishing to show a becoming gratitude to that prosperous time, have never disturbed the appearance or emulated the efforts of that age. So we see old houses with no modern paint whitening their former beauty; lazy fences pointing to the past in every inclination; dead trees adorn the walks; and while the good people sleep on the porches and the old horses doze at the gate, the fly and the beetle hum the self-same music of fifty years ago.

" Within two years, however, some persons ventured upon the enterprise of buying pine land west of here, and hauling the lumber through the town to the railroad. The noise of the wagons woke up the slumbering inhabitants, who from curiosity followed them to the railroad, which they liked so much that they concluded to have one of their own. Hence the march of progress. Potosi has built a branch road to the Iron Mount Railroad, which is about to make a new town of it. This has also aided us in selling our pine woods, now valued at fifty thousand dollars."

" July 5.

" I have been writing to my sister S—— that I cannot go east with her this summer. I wish I could visit her, and home too ; but there will be greater comfort to us both in my staying here, if it is positively my duty, than in indulging in what I ought not.

" Knowing that I was to be here all summer, Mr. H—— and myself have rented a country seat, a very nice one in its way ; an old-fashioned stone house, one and a half stories, with gables, and a little porch over the door covered with vines ; and so we are here embosomed in green, for shade trees hang over us, as the vines creep around us. We are on the river-bank, five miles south of the city, on the edge of the high bluffs which run along the river here; and we get the south breeze as it blows at night, and keep cool, which is the great desideratum.

"We have rented this gem of a place for three months, and call it 'Loafer's Paradise.' If one cannot enjoy what he would, let him enjoy what he can. This principle, if acted upon, would make not only a happier but a better world, for it would save some of the sickly, morbid sorrow which the weakness of human nature is prone to indulge in. I have found it wise to think of what is cheerful in life, and folly to look upon the dark side of the picture."

"August 5.

"In going up town, this afternoon, I saw the dispatch announcing the success of the submarine telegraph. It has made me feel greater and happier ever since. I went for B—— to share my joy, and we proposed that the world should have a jubilee, and that its sovereigns should each drink the health of the other across our ocean, while lightning gave the toasts." .

.   .   .   .

"I read to B—— a review of Buckle's 'History of Civilization,' and, also, from a work on Greece."

12

" September 26.

" I have been very ill of the cholera ; was taken
two weeks ago on board the boat *en route* for
Hannibal.

" I felt ill during the night of September 18th,
and about eleven o'clock, next day, was taken vio-
lently with cramp, my limbs and stomach chilling
at the same time. I called to a gentleman standing near my state-room door to find Mr. P——,
who came immediately, and they, with Mr. H——
and J——, gave me brandy, camphor, and pep-
per, applied mustard, and rubbed me, until they
brought me to life again. The boat soon arrived
at the railroad landing, when Dr. H—— came on
board to see me, and I was soon afterward moved
to the hotel. There I felt comfortable during most
of the afternoon and night.

" On the following morning, about ten o'clock, I
had another attack of cramp, which was more general, and lasted longer than that of the preceding
day. I was very ill for three days, and but just
escaped the third attack of cramp. Still, I had no
fear of dying, and that was my arm of strength.
This is a terrible disease, and justly fills one with
horror. Were it otherwise, no means would be
taken to prevent it, either as a public scourge or

a private ailment, but when an individual is seized with it, there is nothing more fatal than fear."

"September 27.

"A fresh morning with fresh air have come into my room to shake hands with the general freshening which the chambermaid and nurse have introduced inside by means of various devices, from a broom down to a bottle of cologne. All seem so happy and have worked so hard, that I have rallied enough to sit up and write a line, while Mr. R—— has gone out to shoot a bird for my dinner. He has left at the head of the bed, within reaching distance, the table, with the bottle of cologne, beside all the doctor has left there ; and on the pillow, at my left hand, lies my watch, ticking away the time under a perfumed pocket-handkerchief, to make it pass as sweetly as possible. I seize a moment now, while it runs, to record that I have been so sick that once or twice the pulsation of my heart almost ceased its ticking."

"St. Louis, October 9.

"I arrived home yesterday, after an absence of three weeks. The time has seemed long, for during many days of my convalescence I was in just that condition between sickness and health when there was nothing to do but wait; still, I hope the time was not all lost to me.

"I shall ever cherish a grateful remembrance of the kindness I received from all around me, both in the hotel, and also from people in the town. I was delightfully entertained by Mr. L——; in fact, my heart warms at the recollection of the domestic happiness with which he and his family seem surrounded.

"To-day I arose early, and looked after the 'ways of my household,' happy to be here once more. All day my business has seemed easy, and the evening I have spent at home with one of my dear old books."

"Sunday, October 10.

"It was a wet, dismal morning. Mr. P—— came up, and we went to Dr. Post's church. I heard an excellent sermon on the example and grandeur of Christ's character; a theme so lofty, so wonderful, that, when touched by unskilful hands, I am filled with disquiet. The subject of religion is too sacred, too divine, too important, for irreverent lips, or for a man to treat successfully who has naturally but little veneration; and when I hear as I have to-day, and see and feel as I have to-day, the power of God's character so reverently, solemnly, tenderly treated, I am impressed with the greatness of the work of the ministry over any other profession in life.

"After dinner, read the fifth and sixth books of Milton."

" St. Louis, December 5.

" This has been a day of rest from the ordinary vexations and cares of my business, which, although pleasant in itself, involves *so much* care. That is the difficulty. I cannot find the men to execute what I wish to have done with promptness and energy. Well, I have enjoyed the day in reading. Came home early, took the fourteenth, fifteenth, and sixteenth ' *Siécle le Plutarque Français*,' and went to B——'s room.

" We read a little of Cicero, finished ' Marguerite D'Anjou,' and then wound up with the ' Alhambra.' Oh, the Alhambra! the garden of the Lindaraxa and the mysterious chamber! We all were still. We saw the Moorish rose bend its leaves to the Mediterranean winds and drop its fragrance into the Xenil, which bore it through the Vega to the sea. We heard noises in the outer chamber,—the ghosts of the dead who had lain in their graves for hundreds of years,—and we softly barred out the moon, wishing their voiceless spirits peace.

12*

"We read again the legend of the tower of '*Las Infantas*,' and its sequel of the little maiden who afterwards dwelt there, who found the magic lute upon which she played with such masterly skill as to unlock the soul of the would-be dead Philip the Fifth. The maiden and her lute have perished, but the soul of their music still lives, and from the strings of the violin of old Paganini broke forth again the voice of the magic lute.

"Music, music! Whence art thou? From what cause dost thou spring, thou divine, mysterious thing? Who can analyze this art? Who can wish to analyze it? Under its spell the spiritual nature sits, bathed in a heavenly vision, the stern cares of the world are resolved into pleasing pictures, and the absent, the loved, and the lost come to visit us once more."

CHAPTER VIII.

"January 1, 1859.

T has been a cold but pleasant day. Mr. T—— was here betimes, and after making a few calls on foot in the neighborhood, we drove out to Lucas Place, and took our usual New Year's route, dining at home. The principal episode in the afternoon was the appearance of a surprise party of minstrels at Miss P——'s, which frightened the ladies at first as much as they diverted us all afterwards.

"On returning in the evening, found my brother-in-law, Mr. S——, quietly seated reading. We resolved to spend the evening in the same way, but could not find a solitary servant about the place, which made us the more anxious for our tea.

"In looking over the day's visits I do not find much pleasure in it. I review a successful day's business with more satisfaction than any social enjoyment. I do not wish to undervalue what is called social life, and believe I do not, but I would have it progressive. This is the error, — a low standard of amusement. That amusement or entertainment is true, and that only, which will bear reflection; that which in some way is either refreshing to the mind or improving to the taste; which affords rest for the body, a relief from anxiety, a comfort in trouble, or, in other words, that advances our social condition."

" February 15.

" Have had a few days of really interesting, and, I hope, profitable reading. That the original stock of those races which overran and peopled Europe during the early centuries of the Christian era had dwelt in their rude lands for many centuries before we learn their true character by their intercourse with the civilized world, which at that period was Rome, there is but little doubt; that our knowledge of them prior to that time is fabulous, there is none. Yet we must not reject entirely the authority of fable. Song and fable may enlarge a deed, an action, but they cannot create the original idea; and beside, when we analyze beyond by the light of natural laws, we find here and there a bright and true point which lights us back to another.

" That these races were of Asiatic origin, is in accordance with the recognized principle of the migration of nations. This corroborates their national traditions. Their mythology bears a striking similarity to the religion of Brahma, and a still more striking proof of their Asiatic origin is found in the fact that the ancient Sanscrit language of India, which is the classic tongue of that classic Asiatic land, is evidently the origin and mother of not only all the modern, but even the ancient languages. The Sanscrit is now to India what the Latin is to the ritual of the Romish Church, the (vulgarly believed) tongue of the Brahmin Church, which has only been exhumed by recent scholars; and now that the dust of superstitious centuries is dropping away from it, we find modern European languages, Greek and Latin, are classed only as Indo-Germanic tongues."

" March 6.

" As soon as I can possibly arrange to leave my business I shall travel and study, if I am obliged to do it *à la pied*, Bayard Taylor like ; for I need to travel a while or do something to free me from care. I am fatigued, physically and mentally ; my youth will be gone ere I am aware of it, and my manhood will be but a premature old age. A few years of simple, careless life in Southern Europe, with its warm sun and dry air, and the winds which the Mediterranean brings from the desert, will do me much good, and if I live I will see ——

"I have been reading to-day the life of the Emperor Charles V.; and one incident impressed me, showing how much fashionable ladies are indebted to the august Emperor for a favorite *ruse*.

"Charles V. wished Pope Paul III. to call a council at Trent. The Pope would do so if the free cities of Germany would abide by its decision, and Charles knew they would not. When the deputies appeared at court and delivered their articles of refusal and remonstrance, the Emperor received them graciously, and without breaking the seal of the articles or ordering them to be read publicly, thanked the deputies for their humble submission to his wishes, and begging them to bear to his subjects in their several provinces the expression of his good-will, abruptly terminated the audience. The bewildered deputies were sent home, and Charles wrote the Pope to call the council immediately."

.   .   .   .

"On one occasion some of the court ladies were making a call, and from the carriage they saw the ladies of the house seated in the window up-stairs.

Everybody said, ' Oh goodness !' except one young
lady of eminent strategetical abilities, who said,
' Never mind,' and leaping out of the carriage,
rang the bell. ' Ladies in ?' (Servant.) ' Yes,
miss.' (Strategetical lady, in a very loud voice to
be heard up-stairs, handing the cards to the servant.) ' Ah ! very sorry indeed ! Please say to the
ladies, when they return, we are very sorry indeed
we could not see them ;' and they drove off, the
servant still holding the cards, looking very wild.
The ladies of the court quickly copied the style of
convenient misunderstanding, and the fashion has
lived on, though the Emperor has slept in the
dust for hundreds of years.

" It has seemed to me that the court of Charles
V. gave little encouragement to literature, and
that learning was indebted during that long period
to the court of his rival, Francis I., to those inferior princes who acknowledged his nominal
sovereignty, together with the Italian States, and
a portion of the time to the court of Rome. It
seems to me that Charles possessed the very highest order of talent for government, and though
infinitely superior to any prince of his age, except
perhaps Solyman ' the Magnificent,' the fame of his
rivals has been sustained by the favors they be

stowed on men who could but applaud their patrons."

"April 10.

"This week I have been to Potosi, and, what is delightful in the retrospect, had a successful trip.

"The mill we have built will average twelve thousand feet of lumber in twelve hours. There is an ample field in our pine and lead lands for an enterprising man to devote all his energies to, and I wish I could find just the right man to go there. But prompt, energetic, enterprising men are not so easily found. Such characters are raised in the cold, rugged climate of New England, where the barren land drives a man to work during the short summer, else in the long winter he starves.

"Last Friday, my brother arrived with his son Looly. Looly and I are much attached to each other, and we took several rides and walks together. I hope he will develop in manhood as generous a heart and as much energy of character as his father.

"I am now reading Latin three times a week with B——.

"May 8.

"I have, during the last week, been to Castle Rock. On Wednesday, Major C——, Dr. ——,

E—— and myself started down the river in a skiff, the honorable position of helmsman having been assigned to me.

"I acquired an intimacy with the doctor to the extent of persuading him to hold my overcoat as a sail; for which service I recompensed him by a recital of the ancient legends and local traditions of the places we passed, particularly of the haunted house.

"We arrived home at half-past eight o'clock, and this being the week of the fair, I immediately found my way thither. This is a most magnificent fair. The ladies are perfectly charming, which makes the gentlemen perfectly happy.

"To-day, went to church at the Immaculate Conception. Heard Mozart's Grand Mass."

"May 25.

"The thorough, careful study of history seems to be too much neglected in our day by the rising generation. While the young men, particularly in our colleges and schools, should be taught that they have a part, and a great one too, to act in the future, they should also learn to respect the past, and read there the story of our race. Whenever and wherever a race has existed, whether behind mountain fastnesses or locked up by seas, the

13

same human soul has been found working out some form of civilization peculiar to itself, which goes to make up the complete whole of the world's history."

" FOR MY FRIEND'S ALBUM.

" June 12.

" There is nothing in life so dear, either to memory, reality, or hope, as the love which we all bear to our own. I remember that I have had your album far too long, and, startled by the reality, return it now, with the hope that beneath the awakening love which you will bear to your own, as it comes to greet you, all the unpleasant recollections its absence has occasioned may slumber.

" Here, bound and folded among some dry leaves, are the souvenirs of your youthful days, — a quiet grave enough, and fit for new souvenirs to grow over, if carefully tended by the awakening loves of future years.

" May all the endearments of life so cluster around those loves and those years that you may realize therein life's greatest happiness in life's most endearing principle."

" CHICAGO, July 3.

" During the past week I have been very busy every day; no time for recreation; and, in fact, I ask no higher pleasure than that which comes from the successful accomplishment of my business. I heard a lecture one evening on 'Henry Clay,'—a proud theme to an American citizen; and another evening I listened to the same lecturer on 'Europe, from the Fifteenth to the Eighteenth Centuries.' The speaker was evidently a man of genius, but he has not the art of condensing at sufficient command to lecture on so vast a subject.

"Yesterday (Saturday) I left St. Louis for this place; arrived late last evening.

"We have been to church to-day; afterwards, sung. Ah, what a sweet reminiscence singing at Sabbath-evening twilight brings to me! I see my mother always, at such an hour, as she used to appear to me when a child."

"St. Louis, August 18, 1859.

"Dear Parents: I wrote S——, yesterday, that I could not, consistently with my business, leave here now; although I have been hoping all the time that within a few days I should be able to consummate an arrangement which would place me in a position to leave. But it does not turn out so, and I think it best to stay here until fall; then, S—— will be gone, and you will be lonely; so I will try to cheer you, and we will have as happy a

time as we can, and, ordinarily, we can be very
happy if we will.

"I wish I had something good to write. There
is no news to interest you here, except of myself,
and I am getting stale.

"Twenty-seven years old is no new thing;
and though, according to usage, I must say 'I can
scarcely realize it,' yet I do. My life seems long
to me in looking back, and I seem a lucky fellow
all the way; everything in the end comes out for
the best.

"There is one thing in the retrospect that pains
me : I cannot see that my life amounts to anything
further than my personal concerns. I have accomplished nothing, realized nothing, but a little
philosophy of contentment, a spasmodic devotional
sentiment, and an apathetic good-will to my fellows. All this is resolved into an easy-going selfishness, which I fear it is; and a very sorry prospect it is too, for a bachelor of twenty-seven,
in a 'bachelor's hall.' What will it come to at
forty, if I don't get married or do something?
It will come to perfection, and I shall come
to nothing. It is true that I have some native
ability, — I know it and feel it; it is a painful fact
oftentimes ; for I have not sufficient application or
discipline to make it of any avail. Time is not

my slave, I am his. For several years, I have not had the physical strength for constant, earnest application; my cares and responsibilities have been heavy for me; but now, by a proper, prudent course of life, I could study. I have the eyes, and if I had an associate fit to train me, and were free from embarrassments, I would give up my business at once, and pursue some literary avocation. This has been my life-long dream, and I never shall be satisfied with anything else. If I had never seen a book I should have gloried in my business; but business was never to me but the means for an end, and seemed so much the lesser of the two that oftentimes, while dreaming of the end, the means failed to afford me any interest.

"But I do not give up yet; indeed, I hope ere many months to go abroad; and for this purpose have reviewed my Latin the past winter. I am now pretty thoroughly acquainted with French, know something of Spanish, German, and Italian, and shall study them more next winter. After acquiring a basis of modern languages and history, I intend to visit Europe in an humble, quiet way, to study and perfect them; and if I can make any avail of my acquirements, I shall feel proud and happy to do so."

"August 21.

" I have been writing my brother, who is now at St. Petersburg, the locality of which is delightfully suggestive this warm day. I should like to be fanned by the icy breezes which prevail at the northern boundary of that splendid empire, and listen to some of the old Scandinavian ballads of Prince Wladimir and his knights. Ah, yes, there is no end to what the mind suggests which it would like to see in Russia, — but I am not there. The present Emperor is reputed to be a very high-toned man, and on that ground I wrote my brother that I hoped soon to hear that he was closeted with him, from which he would retire with a handsome fortune."

"August 26.

" I have long desired to be of some use to my country ; in fact, this must have been an idea of my childhood, for when I reached years of maturity it seemed an old possession, and although it has never assumed any positive shape, yet there have been many times in my life when it has stood boldly forth.

" When our communities are agitated by the election of prominent officers of government, there is a lack of real patriotism exhibited in the people.

Men of talent, good sense, honor, and reputation quietly fold their hands, and refuse to accept any other duty than that of simply casting their votes; they will have nothing to do with public offices, politics, etc.

" That there is some good reason for such a course by high-minded men, is true, and alarmingly true ; but the fault lies at the door of this same class of men. It took the highest order of talent, the most profound intelligence, the loftiest principle, the most self-sacrificing, conscientious lives, to form our government, and unless it is maintained by the same means, it will, like the proud nations of former times, crumble to atoms.

" That men of no principle, no integrity, no character, no reputation but that of ambitious schemers, have by dishonorable means, in many instances, reached those heights of power which should be occupied only by the greatest minds, augurs no good to our nation. The reckoning time will surely come for this wrong, and we may be called to pay a heavy penalty for it as a people.

" If I ever acquire the education I have so long desired, and if to education is added experience, they shall be devoted in some way to the benefit of my country."

Under date of October 23d, Mr. Boomer, in writing to his mother, gave some of his views of education: —

"DEAR MOTHER: It is now more than a month since your letter came, during which time I have often almost commenced a letter in reply, and oftener still thought about it. There are times, however, when I feel as though I could not do anything except to sit down and think a little, and perhaps read, which is never an effort; but to write easily, or even tolerably well, I must be prepared for it by hard study coupled with reflection.

"I have been led of late to think much of early associations, and the importance of culture in childhood, which is so easily acquired at that tender age, but so difficult comparatively when maturer life creeps on. If pleasantly retained within the influences of home — a religious home — long enough, an ordinary child can easily be made an extraordinary man; for the natural difference of mind, when considered in the aggregate, is but little. The genius of different minds only inclines to different channels, and to develop those inclinations, and build around the mind a proper basis and support, is a high responsibility, as well as a delicate task.

"This noble work belongs to woman. Her sphere is truly great ; and if she successfully accomplishes her work, its benefits will never cease, for the influence of a single mind permeates beyond these fleeting years.

"Now all believe that in a well-balanced mind the defect of one faculty is equalized by the development of another ; and though superiority in one respect may not equal in reputation excellence in another, yet I believe that in its practical bearings upon the welfare of the country it does. I think the principle is becoming much more generally recognized, that a man who attains preëminence in the practical arts of life, has in our times equal esteem with the genius of thought purely ; and we see the effect of it in the practical advancement of civilization.

"I believe, therefore, that if the mother should find in her son a genius for the plough, the loom, or the anvil, she should as assiduously cultivate that inclination as she would one for letters, the bar, or the church.

"Do you not think that the number of children is very few who have not for some sphere in life a peculiar adaptation, a preëminent talent? I believe there are but very few ; and when labor ranks side by side with thought, and when thought

even is dependent upon labor, how foolish, as well
as wrong, is the indolence in which the rising community is growing.

"Labor can always be made pleasant by letting
it be expended in the direction of the inclinations;
and continued accumulated labor applied in one
pursuit will make any man eminent.

"Circumstances may disappoint the best pro-
vision made by the parent, but this has its use in
teaching us that all things are governed by a
higher, wiser Power than that of mind even, and
in cultivating within us a greatness moral and
spiritual, a grandeur preëminent over all others.

"My dear mother, I owe you more than I can
estimate for my early education, for all those points
which constitute character of the highest order
you have never failed to inculcate, either by precept or example.

"Give much love to father.

"Your affectionate son,
"GEORGE."

"September 25.
"It is a source of joy inexpressible, a satisfaction hardly to be realized, that I have fulfilled one
of the plans of my life, although it is a minor one.
I have finished my historical course of reading.

No, that would be arrogating what man can never
say of any part of his work on earth. I should
say that I have executed a plan I laid out years
ago for gaining a general knowledge of history
as a basis for future work. I believe I know
something of this great science from its incipient
stages, and can trace its progress from its dim
beginning, on through the twilight of the first
century to the present time.

" I cannot refrain from saying here that to my
honored and beloved father and mother I owe
much for my love of sacred history. The River
Nile will always speak to me of the infant Moses,
and the touching story of Joseph and his brethren has a more beautiful interest than anything
connected with the grandeur and magnificence of
that once mighty empire, that land of endless research to every thoughtful philosophic mind.

" I have read with care (some I have reviewed)
most of the standard histories, ancient and modern, sacred, military, ecclesiastical, civil, and national. Some of these works are on my shelves
before me. We have been good friends together.
But one day I shall fade away, while they will
live on. St. Louis has a library that will abundantly supply any research in history belonging to
any age or nation. To this public institution I

am greatly indebted, and also to my valuable friends.

" I am so often depressed by the thought that I do nothing with my life, that soon it will be gone, with my work only in anticipation, that I am now encouraged, I am grateful, and will believe in the future that other plans may be consummated, other ends compassed.

" In this hour of my gladness I know of one who will rejoice too, for she loves me truly, womanly, and it will cheer her, for we are brother and sister by blood, more than that by sympathy,— yes, I will write S——, and scold her, by telling her she trifles with her time and talents. But she will know what I mean, and she will love me all the more."

Mr. Boomer was fond of a joke, loved humor and fun, and under their influence writes to a friend : —

" DEAR M.: Before me lies the realization of a beautiful thought. The thought of giving is always beautiful of itself, and must emanate from a mind where beauty asserts her superiority, yet it is but a thought till the act makes it a reality. You gave me three cents (stamped postage), it is before me, and I am thinking of you. How often this little monetary gentleman like what you gave me becomes the realization of beautiful thoughts. In the world of affection, distance, though it cannot sever the connection which stretches away through space binding two hearts together, may yet destroy their language; and how many a thought would sigh unheard behind the prison bars of an isolated mind, did not this little friend, the postage-stamp, come like the old man to the fairies, and bear the pack away steadily over hill and valley, across a sea, maybe, until at the door of another heart he lays the realization of a beautiful thought!

"Now, my dear M——, I imagine you saying that after all the liberality you have bestowed upon me, both in thought and reality, you hope for something in return. This is the very point. On this liberality I ground my faith and build my hope; for that mind which freely gives from its own, does not require a return from another; that kindness of heart which prompts charity will forgive its want in another; and that being which mirrors beauty to all who behold, will not sigh for a counter reflection. So, when I send you my return, it must not be your gift, but one poorer by so much that you will be happy in the contrast,

14

though not profited by the exchange. It shall bear a thought of beauty, for it is of thee. May it reach thee safely, though its transit is not far overland nor across the sea.

"This subject of postage-stamps has reawakened in me the oft-repeated wish that I might be permitted to see some fairy land where women could not talk, and where they could only convey to each other their beautiful thoughts under the seal of three-cent stamps; then I have tried to picture what the proportions of a post-office under such circumstances would assume. It seems to me that it would cover immensity.

"I once had a dream (caused I suppose from indigestion) in which I caught a glimpse of Paradise, and saw a crowd of angels ascending and descending, with great white wings reaching to their feet, hovering about and around a colossal throne. But I must have been mistaken. I think it was a view of that noiseless world where women do not talk, the throne the post-office, the angels, women going in and out watching for the mails, and the wings great white bags of paper on the one side, and on the other postage-stamps.

"Oh, what a blessed land for a poor fellow! I long to go there. I could make postage-stamps, make my fortune, and then go to some other place ; for a man would be rather a silent and lonely individual in such a world for a long time. What would he do ? He couldn't talk, and he couldn't go to the post-office, for there would be no room. He would grow hungry after a time, for he must be a *stationer* in such a land, and the women would bring him for food genius only.

"Dear M——, pardon the good spirits which I am laboring with, not yet having been fed by the ravens of that silent clime. I trust also you will allow me to assure you that, should such be my favored destiny, my heart shall remain as ever yours."

As a friend, no shade of doubt ever rested upon Mr. Boomer's character. A truthful instance of his fidelity may be seen in the following letter : —

"St. Louis, November 30, 1859.

"DEAR H——: I am going to write you. You will not be surprised, I hope ; don't be offended, I pray. I will write with a pencil, whose impression from the page you may easily efface. An angry dash of the hand will do it without trouble. Bring it into contact with another object, and soon it will bear no distinctness or individuality of its own. Should you perchance drop a tear for something or somebody, it will melt the impression easily away; or you may throw it aside, or fold it by as a thing of an hour, and time will dim it, till it becomes but a shadow of the page.

"So I sacrifice this pencil to oblivion, with no truer motive than that it shall share a kindred lot with my own fate; and it affords me pleasure now perhaps to anticipate that when we both get to oblivion together I may pick it up again, and be happy for an hour; for I have come to believe that an angry moment has without trouble dashed my impression from a page brighter, more endur-ing, and one which God made purer far than this, the page of your brilliant existence, — that hav-ing been brought into contact with other objects, my impression has lost all distinctness.

"When the world forgets us our existence must maintain itself in oblivion. When one being is to us more than all the world beside, and that being holds our remembrance no more, our poor life is left to oblivion. You may forget me, dear H——, and so in that gloomy land I shall awake to find its melancholy walls overshadowed on every side.

"I will trouble you no more with my stupid fancies, but will say a few ill-natured things, that are prompted by no ill-natured heart.

"I have ever been and will be your friend, though never so by the flattery of your faults, which, if indulged too freely, will undermine the basis of your highest and noblest superiority as a woman. My dear H——, you have from childhood had no one to take you kindly by the hand and point to you that humble, quiet path which leads to a 'jewelled throne.' You wandered alone too young in the valley of life, and merging into womanhood, you were admired, flattered, and adored. Yet, though deceived, your lofty spirit can brook no superior even of imposition, and you have sometimes deceived in return. The impetuosity of your nature has carried you too far, and, thoughtlessly, to witness the workings of another heart, you have deceived that heart.

"These are the time-killers and vain amusements of an unsatisfied, restless life; for your life is unsatisfied; it has nothing commensurate with its capacity, and the true greatness of your nature is seldom awakened; but when it is, no petty deceit is shown; far from it; truth, noble truth, flashes in every thought and action. Yet beware, for heaven's sake, my dear H——, beware, for circumstances and habit — that tyrannical creature habit — may triumph over nature, so that after a few spasmodic throes it lies prostrate and bound

14*

in the chains of her minions. So petty deceits, urged on by an unsatisfied, unhappy life, may cover truth so deep that, after a time, a few convulsive efforts will alone indicate the existence of that on which God built the structure of human greatness and human love, and which the enemy of all good dared alone steal away.

"I know, my dear H——, that you have that greatness of character which will enable you to regulate your actions as at will, and I pray you as a friend to consider what I have said. If I have told you truth, act upon it as your heart will dictate, and I shall behold in you a heroism greater than I have yet witnessed, yet one of which I have always believed you capable, — a heroism grander by far than the world has handed down through her ages of history and song, — the heroism of conquering one's self. If it is not truth, tell me so, kindly, as a friend, and I shall owe you a thousand pardons a thousand times. You may remember that on one occasion you asked me to tell you your faults; I have done so, and have told you all that I consider worthy the name, frankly, freely. You will tell me if I have been wrong, and I will never speak or breathe a word of them again, and you may rest assured that to other than you I never have. On one occasion I told you some things in a manner I should not have done; this I truly regret, and beg you will forgive.

"I may often talk indifferently, but I pray you to believe me your friend, though a strange one; and should an opportunity offer, God knows that my friendship will bear the test."

CHAPTER IX.

LOVE.

R. BOOMER was never married, but the following touching record bears ample testimony to the fact that he had "loved and lost:"—

"It is said that '*man's* love is of his life a part.' Man's love! Is it not as real an element in his character as of woman's? I believe that from this part of his nature emanate the springs of his happiness, — his ambition, his hopes, his expectations, and, in fact, his entire earthly condition. Blot out this passion, and, like the going down of the sun, which darkens all the landscape around, the future of life is walled in by an impenetrable darkness, and all joy seems stricken from the past.

"I am sitting here in my arm-chair, at midnight, before the waning coal fire; my eyes are looking steadily, though vacantly, for something dim, faint, and distant in the air, that must have hidden itself

or dropped away in the dying embers. Perhaps it
is a phantasy, but I think it is my soul which has
fled, and is now wandering far beyond where spec-
tres wane in the firelight. So it has gone and
left me here alone, like some ruined old house-
walls, the occupant fled, and my eyes, looking so
fixedly on the fading firelight, like two old win-
dows in the crumbling house-tower, peering out
upon the gloomy evening as it steals over the receding daylight.

"My soul has fled! Alas! Oh, no; I laugh at
the thought. Now a stealing smoke, now a flash-
ing flame, bursts out from a smouldering coal and
leaps away into air, and I think how beautiful and
kind it would be could my soul, too, burst its char-
nel-house, and leap away far behind its dingy bars
into air, the spirit-land, where it may look kindly
upon me from the 'isles of affection,' which the
Loves have chosen as their abode.

" How many fancies chase each other through
the shadowy chambers of my mind, ever fitful, yet
ever constant; ever circling in the airy pathway
of the soul, as the fancies of the lingering day
chase each other out from the shadowy chambers
of its night-home. And the gray old ruin, the
broken home, it seems constant to its soul (as I
would be); for there it stands on the hill at mid-

night, and stares with its vacant eyes through the
long night into the silent western sky. It seems
to be vainly watching for its departed spirit, which
gave it life and sunshine, and twined around its
tottering strength some tender ivy with hale affection for its passing years. As it gazes so silently
through the night-hours, it seems to say, 'Old
world, send up a bright gleam now and then, and
we will see each other ere long crumbling away
together; but while we are here let us hope, and
hope ever. Though our life is gone with our soul,
we can see its shadow as it dances on the vacant
air in the light of yonder moon.' So I sit here
silently, at midnight, staring upon the smouldering fire before me, and say, 'Old fire, we are one;
we are dropping away together; send up a bright
gleam now and then, and we will see how fast we
are going.' I will stare away, though my life is
gone with my soul, while its shadows dance before
my eyes by the light of you flickering lamp. But
I pray them away. I mourn my soul; for it gave
me life and sunshine, and stirred some pleasant
memories, and would, I hoped, entwine for me,
in my deserted home, some hale affection for my
passing years. Maybe it will come again in the
morning, when the shadows hie them from their

wassail rout, and then it will tell its evening tale of sadness.

"Another night, at midnight, and I sit here over the dead ashes that cover the coals (for I have buried them deeply, and shall leave them alone), and dead as the ashes, with a fiercer flame covered within, which is buried deep, and leaves me alone, I gaze, and muse, and dream of the story of my soul. It must go from me no more, for it makes me sad with my destiny. It came to me last night, as I slept in my arm-chair, and said, 'There is a way yonder; do you see, through the darkness, the Valley of Life ?' I fly there when night drapes down from the mountain-tops the funereal robes of day. I go down behind these mountains, and ride on the wings of the sun.

"When the first shadows of night appear, a little valley peeps up, gently reaching back to the hills. All is beauty, native, wild, among flowers and trees and mossy rocks and pleasant turfs ; and here the souls of men spring up as pure, wild, and free as is the birthplace of the wild valley.

"Nature weeps here at night over this her infant child, and bathes it with many tears; but as the sun comes up they trickle down the hills, the turfs sparkling, the flowers laughing as they go, and down the valley they run away together, forming the River of Life.

"On down the valley goes, on down the river runs, and each grows broader and smoother and deeper, and both grow darker as they press on.

"Plains roll away with them to the forests, and forests over plains and hills, clustering beneath the mountains, whose blue peaks rise above in the sky. Bare and cold rocks stare down upon it from their summits, precipices frown on it, abysses yawn over it, while the waters sweep down through all, and swell the great River of Life.

"Fields and meadows, cities and towns, and the men therein, all mingling, seem to ride first here, then there, upon the chariots of the storms that rush out from their vast caves beneath the mountains, to attack and affright the world.

"But when the spirits of peace come from their homes in the heavens and scatter the storms and bind them up in their prisons, I see the valley again; fainter and fainter it appears, till but a barren shore of the great sea is seen, with the River of Life rolling feebly on. The stream becomes sluggish and ebbs on lower, slower, and slower, lower, till the waves of eternal waters surge over it, the eternal mists come up, and the 'Valley of Life' is gone.

"It is said that long ago God called together all the spirits of men, and showed them this 'Valley of Life,' and said, 'Behold the pathway to eternal rest. Go, travel through the valley, but do not linger wistfully by the way, nor wander in its treacherous paths, which will lead you astray, but follow down by the quiet river, so that when you cross the great waste, and tread solitarily the arid sands that stretch away to the sea, you may partake of its waters; and if you reach the shores of the great sea in safety, ere the waves dash over you, the mists will bear you over to the Isle of the Blessed, around whose base may dash unheeded the billows of eternal years.'

"Once I travelled through the valley; and now my story. Life opened for me propitious enough (as for all). The world had laughed in the sunshine, twilight was softening the din of day into the hum of evening, when a pale star shone out before all the rest, clear and cold. In my baby dreams I must have seen the star, so pale, so clear, gleam upon the shadowy wall where the night-lamp flickered, and the darkness crept away in the corners.

"In boyhood I saw it through the trees, ere the moon rose, before the old gabled house; but in spite of my fear of it, and the stories that were

15

told me of ghosts that came like stars, I loved it
even then, and was happy, for I was free, and
romped with the boys at school, and roamed alone
through woods and fields, and by the brook that
ran down from the hill covered with pines.

"One night in autumn I went there, and sat
down in the shade of the scattered pines. The
moon shone down among them, and the autumn
winds sighed among their tops. I loved to hear
the winds sigh and the brooks murmur, and to look
upon the heavens, and be still. On that night the
breathings of the air were so soft that it seemed
to hush my own, and I watched the noiseless
clouds moving about among the stars, like great
white armies, with their chariots and cloudy steeds
and horsemen all draped in tattered robes, with
tattered banners fringed with fairy forms. At
last they gathered thick and dark and still over
the moon ; darkness rushed to the forest, and
the tree-tops hushed their sighs. I shuddered, but
still looked upon the clouds, for they were moving
off from the moon, and stood over my star, which
had been looking upon me from its far-off home in
the sky. I pitied the star, for it always seemed
alone ; but I loved it too, and called it mine, and
had often indulged the thought that when I died
my home would be there, that my friends would

be there, and that there would be my heaven; and now, thought I, the clouds are going to hide it from its little friend; but it was only for a moment, and they moved away.

"The tissue clouds moved up and down, till I saw written in my star, as clear as the heavens, the cold word, 'Alone!' A meteor shot across the sky, and, dropping behind a cloud, out came in fiery letters the word 'Alone!' A blast sprung out from the north, and driving through the pines, with hoarse voice said, 'Alone!' And the brook even, as it went rippling on, murmured out 'Alone! alone!' I buried my face in my hands and cried, 'Alone! alone!' for I had read my horoscope, 'Alone!' in the stars.

"I rose to go home, but hours after it seemed to haunt me, that I was, and was to be. a boy, a man, alone in the world; and the star looked kindly upon me no more, for it had said 'Alone!'

"What a cruel thing is destiny! What a cruel thing is thought! Day and night, anywhere, everywhere, it holds us at its will, and makes us happy or drives us mad.

"Well, anon. Long years since then are gone. I went away to school, and through seven years, among a hundred boys, I was a boy alone. I went away to business, and four years more I travelled, sometimes, indeed, alone, but always 'alone.' I went to a city to live, and five years more, among a hundred thousand people, I lived alone. One day I met another, and I thought I would be alone no more. I saw her often, and never was alone again anywhere. Everywhere she was with me. I had found a friend, I thought, and was happy. I went away from my home, and on returning found my friend was becoming more than a friend to me; and then I thought of my destiny. Alas! our destiny! It is a fearful thing.

"One night in October I saw her; the winds sighed through the trees, the autumn blasts whistled, and clouds, as light and restless as tissue, were gathering, and as I saw them standing over her, who was dearer far to me than the star of my boyish days, I shuddered, for as they tore away I saw written there the cold, clear word, 'Alone!' A flash of fire burst from my heart and wrote, in fiery letters, 'Alone!' A blast swept through the trees that said, with dismal voice, 'Alone!' The breathing of the air seemed to murmur, 'Alone! alone!' I buried my thoughts in my bosom, for I had read my horoscope, 'Alone,' in my heavens; and that night, though none knew it, I went to my home a wretched man.

" What a cruel thing is destiny! What a cruel

thing is thought! Day and night, anywhere,
everywhere, it holds us at its will, and it makes us
happy or it drives us mad. . . . .

"For months I have acted a scene hollow
enough, yet terribly real. A laugh may ring out
merry and loud, but ere it dies away echo will
catch it up, and from some hollow chamber of the
heart will ring it out again, shrieking with mimic
sounds. I believe the love of a true man to be
no trifling thing. I feel myself to tremble under
a feeling powerful enough to be conquered only
by death, or, what is worse, by the extinction of
the affections of my nature.

"Thank God, this bitter cup is never to be
drunk but *once* in man's life, and I thank him, too,
that I have an iron will, that can lead me at its
choice, though I hear the clank of its chains and
see its bars across the light. . . . .

"Love and I have sworn eternal warfare. It
was almost a cruel oath, for often, within the
prison where I have encased my heart, I hear it
moan, and sometimes, when the sunshine of a
happy day sparkles through its bars, it glistens
on a tear. . . . . . .

"For a long time, unconsciously, I have loved,
as I have always loved, the image of truth, whether
it burst from nature's passions, or whether it lie
15*

deeply hidden among her virtues, and where, unseen to the eye, the heart alone hears a music stealing ever, ever on, so eloquently pleading that, as
in a dream, it is stolen away.

"This has been no dream, no delusion; it has
been and is a reality, a bitter joy. I have called
upon the cold demi-god, Reason, to help me overcome this unequalled sorrow; but no, it binds me
fast. I cannot as yet break or loosen its fetters.

"I will bury it deep, deep! and I will go out
into the world with my usual calmness. None
shall know, save one, of that deep grave. But I
will wait in patience; I will call upon endurance;
and maybe, in after years, flowers will spring
from this grave, and shed a fragrance over my
future lot."

CHAPTER X.

R. BOOMER had laid his plans to bring his business to a close in the year 1859, and go to Europe, for travel and study. This had been a fixed purpose from his second year's residence in St. Louis, and to meet that end he had overworked himself physically and mentally. His journal bears record of lessons, in different languages, learned in railroad cars and on board steamers, and recited under every difficulty; in fact, not a daily entry is made but something is accomplished with a book.

But perilous times were drawing near, and he was obliged to defer his European plans of study, which he doubtless never abandoned. Whatever was his disappointment at delay, he seemed to believe that the future was destined, in some way to fulfil to him his life-long hope.

Like many other men, he had been dazzled by his success, and was anxious to be independent of business for other purposes. He had entered

into it too largely for the threatening times, which
hung like leaden clouds over the State of Missouri. Had the commercial prosperity of the
country been uninterrupted, his plans would have
been pleasant and profitable. He had identified
himself with the interests of Missouri, and in
going abroad for an indefinite period he wanted
still a hold upon the dear State of his adoption,
— some place he could call home. Therefore, to
build up manufacturing interests, and retain some
share in them, would be a strong link in the chain
of his life, — something to which he could right-
fully return.

In order that he might better surmount the difficulties in which he was entangled, he removed his
home temporarily to Castle Rock; or, to use his
own words, "I have a large property there and
in the vicinity, which I can no longer afford to
neglect; and my other business is so arranged
that I can attend to it by being here a part of
the time. This will give me the care of my saw-
mills, flour-mills, my farm, my rents, and my property at the mouth of the Osage."

He wrote one of his sisters that he had moved
into the country to enjoy the quiet, independent
life of a farmer; which called forth a letter of in-

quiry and remonstrance on her part, which he evasively and humorously answered : —

"DEAR S——: I answer yours before I get cold. I would say 'it' (meaning the letter), but it seems unkind to impute cooling propensities to so kind a letter ; and so, though winter wanes, and some spring blossoms have come, and the air breathes milder, I intimate that there yet remains within me Boreal tendencies. Why not ?

"'If we did not keep cool we should spoil,' *on dit;* and I beg you to believe that if I end this letter with a sentiment which shall somewhat redeem that part of it which I am confident you will pronounce spoiled in the making, I shall in doing so be very cool ; and by this I mean simply to say, that if I subscribe myself 'your affectionate brother,' I shall understand what I am saying, and *shall be* your affectionate brother, and always expect, in a greater or less degree of temperature, to be the same.

" This declaration of attachment, at the close of this letter, will comprehend the past, present, and future, covering the entire period of my life. By this I mean to tell you that my affection is a living principle. This principle is often expressed, in a business-like way, at the close of a letter, by 'ever yours,' etc., and should you prefer this practical ending, I offer to adopt it in future; and I hope you will give the matter serious consideration, for the ending of a letter is like the last greeting of a friend, — it betrays the thought uppermost of all others; it is like the last lingering look thrown over the landscape of the affections.

"I am right well; am at Castle Rock much of the time, busy with all the departments of industry belonging to my dear little town. The house I am temporizing has not princely apartments, but it has a library, with books, and piano, and plenty of easy-chairs, with this writing-table which is now being devoted to your interest. It has a dining-room you would find very useful, which, with your sleeping apartments, will be all you need know anything about. Separated from this dwelling, I have stables, where my horses and cows and working animals maintain an easy, happy life. The horses are gentle; we could roam through the woods, now filled with wild flowers in their first bloom; the boats are plying up and down the river, which is filled with wild fowl; and I will show you how to shoot them, and give you my faithful Zip to bring to your feet the dead and wounded. Don't you think you could spend a month happily here, with your brother, 'in the country?'

"But I would not want you to come now, for you are at home with mother, and for her sake I wish I were there with you; but as it cannot be, I am truly glad you are there, and won't say much of the reality of things here, as 'all's well that ends well.'

"Give my dearest love to mother, and then to father, and you take the balance, which I think may be divided and still leave me

"Your affectionate brother,

"GEORGE."

During this year, 1860, he wrote few letters to his friends, and his journals simply narrate that he was at Castle Rock or St. Louis, where he still kept his office, with the business incidents of the day.

Under date of April 20th, he says:—

"It is a bright, fresh morning. I have been sitting in my room. Mailed a letter to B——; after which read Harper's review of foreign affairs, and the notes on the death of Irving. What a year for the departure from this earth of men illustrious in literature,—Prescott, Irving, and Macaulay, men who have stamped their impress on the world's best age, and reproduced some faithful pictures of the past.

.   .   .   .

"I do not like to write much about these times, — will let my memory serve."

The friend B——, to whom Mr. Boomer alludes in the journal just noted, was in Europe. He had been a tutor as well as friend, and the following extracts from his letters develop the plans they had formed together: —

"BERLIN, December 18, 1859.

"DEAR BOOMER: Shall I see you before the end of 1860? The inner life is very pleasant here, truer and more genial than in France; and, besides, it is such a seat of learning, at least for the studies in which I take the most interest. How is it with your German? It is worth the pains you may take in acquiring it, but remember, for travelling purposes, French will take you through the world. I shall hereafter send you a little piece of a letter every two or three weeks, but I was scarcely settled enough in my mind to do so the first few months. You will understand what I mean when you come over yourself."

Six months later, from the same place : —

"DEAR BOOMER: I am heartily sorry for the temporary pressure you experience in your business affairs; still, I have confidence in your power of management, and have no doubt that all will come out well in the end. Your trip to Europe will only be thereby delayed for a while, that's all. We may yet meet each other on the 'Boulevard des Italiens,' or stroll arm-in-arm through the park of Versailles. . . . .

"It is to lead the life of a God almost, this student life in Germany, — to hear day by day the most distinguished men in the land lecture, and condense in a short hour the result of a long life of study: Droyson and Ranke and Niedner in history, Bopp for Sanscrit, etc., etc.; more than one hundred and fifty professors to choose from.

"And then the stage here, art, the museum, and the private collections! I feel that I shall soon long for rest; there is too much, too much for a lifetime.

. . . .

"Good-by, my friend. If you have as much confidence in yourself as I have in you, you will never feel 'discouraged,' as you tell me in the letter that is before me."

16

"PARIS, September 18, 1860.

"DEAR BOOMER: I believe I last wrote you from Heidelberg. I have been wandering since then more than I could begin to tell you.

"You inform me that I have been appointed Professor of Modern Languages. I must decline it. I shall remain here for the present, where I study and teach.

"And you, why don't you come? I'll be the best Cicerone for you in this glorious old place. You don't even say now, as in former letters, that you will be here at all. What does it mean? If you are coming, now is your time; and it needs very little money, when one goes rightly about it. Paris even, which is one of the most expensive places in Europe to live in, is yet, to one who lives as a stranger in the Hotel du Louvre, or any such place, very cheap compared to St. Louis, and Germany is still cheaper. Come and try life here for a while, and if you do not stay some time then I have mistaken you.

"If you do not come, you ought to let me send you some books; for I hope you read French often, and do not neglect your German; and if you want more books I shall be glad to get them, or do anything else for you I can.

"It is winter here, and I sit by my anthracite

fire, thinking over the plans we once made together. I am sorry if it has been and is to be but
a dream. Come, my ambitious friend, rouse up
that divine spark which I saw gleaming within you
a few times as you talked of future projects, of
life-long hopes. It was the expression of such
sentiments which made me feel that I had found
one who had the ability to ascend into the highest
realities of life. Eh! what are a few dollars more
or less? By the way, I have learned half-a-dozen
new languages since I have been in Europe, and
feel that I have done more in the last nine months
than I should have done in almost as many years
in America.

"Good-by, still hoping I may press your hand
in the shadow of the Tuilleries.

"Your friend,   F——— B———."

It is painful for those who knew Mr. Boomer
well to dwell upon this year of his life, for they
only who thoroughly understood the strength of
his character could appreciate the greatness of his
disappointment.

He never talked of himself, of his aims, or his
griefs, except to those whose right it was to know,
and even then reluctantly. His sensibilities were
keen, and he sought to protect them by an indiffer-

ence or philosophy of which it was said he possessed abundance. No person could look with greater contempt than he upon morbid sentimentalism, that fictitious melancholy which delights in "querulous ecstasy of woe," that lack of true manliness which flies from difficulties, and refuses to bear with a courageous heart the ills of life as they come.

During the Presidential campaign of 1860 Mr. Boomer gave much thought to the conflicting questions then threatening the country, and fearing greatly that misfortunes of a sad character were in store for us, he entreated his friends to look at the condition of things in their true light, and to act wisely for their own interests and the cause of humanity.

Among the candidates for the President's chair he looked upon Mr. Douglas as the man best fitted to harmonize the discordant elements, and he gave to him and the party he represented his hearty coöperation.

The following are extracts from an address delivered at a Democratic convention in the summer of 1860. The place and date were not recorded.

" It is said by wise men, historians, statesmen, and philosophers, that all forms of government, in

all ages and climes, have been, and (the inference
is) will be corrupt; that consequently politicians,
men who hold posts of office, are easily contami-
nated. This becomes an indisputable fact from the
observations of every individual, and in exact
proportion to his intelligence.

"We are possessed of corrupt natures; perfect
equity is not the natural child of sin; and the injustice arising from men collectively seems often
aggravated. But allowing this to be true, is that
any reason why men should not be honest with
their consciences, or act inconsistently with their
intelligence in choosing public rulers? On the
ground that there is wrong in the world, and that
it will never be extinct, shall we consciously aid in
swelling the tide of vice? This stream is already
broad enough, and it becomes our duty as upright
men to throw into its poisonous waters all the
counteracting influence in our power, else it may
deluge our fair land, and we ourselves be swept
into some vortex of ruin.

"I believe there can be (we all know there
should be) a firm, settled principle of action in
our public affairs, and I call upon you all, fellow-
citizens, to stand immovably by the truth. To accomplish this object, I beg of you, as true friends
of our country, to lay aside every personal

consideration of ambition, prejudice, party, — of friends, of differences past or differences expected, even so much of honest opinion as may seem to conflict with the same sentiment in others in such a degree as to impair the general good, and unite upon the man who loves his country, and who will stand by it in the hour of danger.

.   .   .   .

"I have but little to say concerning the bearing which this election will have upon the State, of which every good citizen should remember that he is an integral part. I shall assume that every one whom I have the honor to address holds, next to his religion and his allegiance to his common country, the love and welfare of the State of which he is a sovereign member. In appealing to this principle, I appeal directly to your highest individual interests; for as in the body corporate each integral part develops or withers in exact ratio of the condition of the whole, so in the body politic the individual member sinks with the depression of the times and rises with the general prosperity.

"The misfortunes of the State are those which bow down the man. War, pestilence, famine, civil strife, corruption, and financial distress, are not the creations or misfortunes of individuality or of petty communities, but the miseries of the State, which reach to and bow down the least and humblest of its members. The proof of this is and has been exhibited in every sovereign community, be it barbarous, enlightened, or civilized. Their system of government, their policy, external and internal, their laws, their public institutions, monuments and improvements, will exhibit in each and every instance a faithful representation of the condition of the people.

"The Egyptians, a type of the earliest nations of civilization, built pyramids of colossal proportions in the valley of the Nile, which for four thousand years have withstood the ravages of time, and with alike indifference have looked down upon the storms of the sea and the storms of the desert, and in these monuments alone we may behold a striking picture of Egyptian society as the civilization of that age.

.   .   .   .

"What is our Union of to-day? 'The United States of America,' a full-grown man in the family of nations, which our brethren, full of the instincts of our greatness, have shortened and intensified into the one word 'America,' — that signifies a continent whose confines touch the oceans, and reach from the polar sea to the equator.

"But neither men nor nations, continents, hemi-

spheres, or spheres, are full grown, except by that
law of creation which, from vital forces in the
smallest particles, by growth develops, materially
or spiritually, until they compass the ends which
original wisdom has designed for them. So our
country, from the feeblest beginnings, by a vital
force, by a most rapid development of the law of
growth, has come to our present state, and has
answered, so far, in her influence upon the world,
no inconsiderable or ignoble end."

In the summer of this year Mr. Boomer made
his last visit home before entering the army, — a
visit full of interest, and of which he made de-
tailed memoranda.

" August 22, 1860.

" ' Homeward bound.' Left yesterday for St.
Louis, *en route* to visit my early home. On the
train I met Major W——. Our acquaintance was
singular. We were both standing on the last plat-
form of the train, admiring and remarking, half to
ourselves, half to each other, the beautiful effect
of the sunset mingling with the smoke which
hung over the city. I shall never forget it, so
it is useless to describe it here. We went on
from the sunset to the smoke; then to the manu-

factories that produced it, to their artisans, their rents, their landlords, the landlords' per cent., property taxes, and the material condition, both in reality and prospect, of St. Louis. Afterward we talked of politics, of men, of literature. It was one of the pleasantest conversations of my life."

" September 6.

"I left my acquaintance at Columbus next day, *en route* for Baltimore, while I went to Cleveland, where I arrived at three o'clock, P. M., finding no one but Mr. S—— at home. My sister and the children had preceded me by a few days to Worcester. I left Cleveland the same evening in the boat, went directly to New York, and from there to Worcester *via* Norwich. I reached home Saturday morning, about the break of day. My mother met me at the door. I had not seen her for three years.

> " ' My mother ! at that holy name
> Within my bosom there's a gush
> Of feeling which no time can tame, —
> A feeling which for years of fame
> I would not, could not crush ! '

"My father I found in the garden. Three years have told upon him, — his reverend locks are

whiter. Yes, three years have left an impress
there. My father is sixty-six; I am twenty-eight.
Should I reach his period in life, it might tell a
sadder story for me; would that it might tell as
good a one. But life is hope, and hope is life.
Ara and Bella came next, full of glee that Uncle
George had come; after a little, just at breakfast,
S—— came, looking ——. Well, she is my sister.

"Oh, how blessed to be home once more! This
is my longest absence from it, and I feel to shake
all cares and business from my mind, and, unbur-
dened, yield myself to perfect content.

"The following day, being the Sabbath, we all
went to church in the morning, to hear Mr. Way-
land; in the afternoon S—— and I went to Dr.
Hill's.

"On Monday, S——, Ara and Bella, and myself,
went to Attleborough. Johnny met us at Paw-
tucket with the carriage. There had been a rain,
and this, combined with the richness of the late
summer,

> "'When there is on the leaf a browner hue,
>   And in the skies a deeper blue,'

made our ride of eight miles a delightful one.
We gave ourselves up to unrestrained enjoyment
at the beautiful summer home of my elder sister.

We were now in-doors, now out of doors, giving full license to the play of our affections; yet I could but think of the sadness which had been felt under that roof, for five lovely children had been gathered from it by the reaper Death, two only of the seven remaining. I looked at my sister often, wondering at her Christian fortitude. After tea we went into the grove in the rear of the house, and I cannot paint in words the beauty of the rustic pond there, with the little mounds reaching down to its winding shore, bearing tall trees to hang over it, which held swings, made shade, and let in patches of the setting sun. There was a little boat on the pond, about as long as Johnny is tall, but he seated himself in the stern with a paddle, and little Ara he placed in the opposite end, and as still as air they paddled along. My sisters and Bella and Amelia and I all seated ourselves on the big rock from which the tiny boat was launched, and we all laughed and cried, 'Hurrah for Johnny!' and I embraced the children, thinking all the while how beautiful it was.

"On Tuesday I bade good-by to my dear sister and family at Attleborough, and returned to Worcester. For the remainder of the week I was half sick with chills. It was not very unpleasant, how-

ever, being a comfortable invalid under such circumstances.

"Sunday morning I drove S—— down to our
childhood's home in Sutton, where my father
preached so many years. We took the old road
through the centre of the town, and arrived at
the church just in time for the service.

"The localities seemed scarcely changed, and
many faces bore the impress of time so lightly
that fifteen or twenty years seemed a little while
to me. Old Mr. Cole,—blind Stephen Cole,—that
good, pathetic face has only grown more classic
and grand by the years that have intervened since
I said my catechism to him in the high, square
pew, from which the window looked out upon Mr.
Crossman's orchard.

"My father was in the pulpit, as he used to be
when I was a boy, and in the afternoon he was
eloquent. He has lived a long life, eloquent in
truth, in conscientious adherence to moral and religious principle.

"They have changed the pulpit and the church
inside; they have taken away the square pews
and the galleries. I wish they had let them alone,
for the old faces did not sit where they ought to
have sat, and the new ones had no place in my old
church of twenty years ago.

"After service S—— and myself walked in the grave-yard. We used to go there when children. There are more graves now.

" We drove with father past our house of years ago, but there have been so many changes made upon it, and another house has been built so near, that I could not bear to look at it. All that is left untouched is the front door and knocker. The lower orchard seemed nearly the same; by the brook all looked the same, although my favorite pear-tree was dead and cut down.

" There was a third service at five o'clock, and on returning from it S—— and myself had an earnest conversation, amounting almost to a discussion, on the comparative merits of city and country life. S—— was enthusiastic for the country, as she always was, and on that day everything had conspired to arouse her religious sentiment. I advocated the city, in all its practical bearings, very calmly. It seemed a beautiful ending to the day, which had been one of great interest,— more than I could possibly express, — and which, of itself, compensated me for the journey home. It was one of those experiences that never come a second time in man's life.

" Monday, at four P. M., I said good-by to home."

17

The pleasantest reflection Mr. Boomer had from this visit was the thought that his parents were independently situated in their declining years; and to his mother he writes: "I think of you and my father often, and am so glad to know that you have a quiet, cheerful home in your old age, — a home, though removed from your children, yet among or near the friends of your youth, those days when your life was labor more than now.

"The thought of your home, its permanency, peace, quietude, gives to all of us, your children, more happiness than it does to you, I fear. Realizing what are blessings to you in your declining age, and contrasting them with the situation of some of your children, who are sometimes baffling with and sometimes riding on the tide of the world, and always along with it, you are too apt to think we are unfortunate in the comparison; and this, I have no doubt, often pains you, feeling that your children have not so happy a lot as yourself.

"This is all wrong. We are so constituted by education (practical I mean) and circumstances that it would be cruel almost to give us the lot you sometimes wish us. We have lived long with the busy world, and though we have seen many vicissitudes of fortune in it, still it has never done us harm of itself, but has, I hope, taught us some good; therefore we love it. I am certain that every one, in almost any situation in life, is just as happy and contented as he has within himself the capacity to be. Thus I am impressed with the idea that we all have something to do in life for ourselves, and for those who live with us, and whatever falls to our lot to do, to do it should be our greatest pleasure.

"I believe I am as happy in performing my present duties as I can be, unless, by becoming better or greater, new springs of happiness would be opened out for me; and few things can teach truth and love, to those wishing to learn in a practical sense, better than the great world in which we live."

CHAPTER XI.

THE PATRIOT.

"January 1, 1861.

THE New Year! The phrase does not seem to startle a solitary thought from what I feel within me to be almost a sluggard's slumber. It falls upon my ear absolutely flat, meaningless, joyless, griefless, listless. I do not know why, but as a point in time it has no meaning beyond the hour of the day or the day of the week. My 'New Years' have heretofore been mostly spent in the city, in such a manner as to awaken memories of former ones; and so I have looked back on those days as rounds that I have grasped from year to year in the ladder of my life. The ladder for the last year has been in a horizontal position, and I have just held on."

It is evident that the first months of 1861 were to Mr. Boomer months of fiery trial, that he was passing through a terrible conflict, and that he sometimes felt that he was fighting his way alone.

Born and brought up in Massachusetts, a State which had always taken extreme views upon the subject of slavery, he had heard and seen many things (as has been previously noticed) which were, he maintained, unjust to the South and aggressive on the part of the North, — views which, if carried out, would certainly lead to difficulty. He always begged of his friends in the New England States to try to look at the subject from the slaveholder's point of view, and urged that hatred and violence would never convict men of a moral evil. Moreover, he abhorred quarrels, and in private life acted upon the principle of never contending. If he had disagreement with any person, he simply declared his position, but never used any means to vindicate his course; acting upon the common-sense principle of forgiving wrongs and letting them alone.

A letter, under date of January 6, will give some idea of the workings of his mind upon this subject: —

" DEAR S——: I did not receive the letter you say you wrote, and the postmaster does not know anything about it either. And the beautiful young lady, — they (the young ladies) are myths sometimes ere you catch them, and I believe your letter

mythical. Send me the counterfeit and let me see
(the young lady I mean), and then I can tell
exactly what the letter would or should have been,
and you can write me a letter about something that
is real; for we have in our times plenty of realities, and, though they are sad ones, they are ours.

"We (I mean the people) have been working
hard and long to get them, and, now that they are
in our possession, the inquiry begins to dawn upon
our awakening senses much as it did upon that
young man who drew an elephant in the lottery,
the story of which you know. I think we are
much in the same condition as that perplexed
young gentleman. The elephant is stirred up,
sure enough, and I am afraid he will eat us all up.
I wish, though, I had charge of him for a while ;
I would feed him on corrupt politicians till he
died.

"I wish you (I trust you did have) a merry
Christmas and a happy New Year's day, and wish
for the rest a happier ending than beginning of
this new year.

"I cannot try to cheer you or myself with the
solace that comes to us in individual trials, when
perhaps our greatest troubles are our highest
hopes, and when we may reflect with pleasure
that if our burdens are great we are lightening the

load for another ; for there is no hope in madness, and it goes down from father to son.

"You do not know how much I am weighed down by these evil times ; you cannot conceive it, living where there is a union of feeling. You are on the border, where the realities of civil strife do not appeal to you as they do to us here, who may be occupying the theatre of fearful tragedies, our whole State a battle-ground. If you did, if the far North and the far South could hear the prospective cries of distress that come to our ears, and see through the medium we do, they would come to the conclusion, I think, that there had been a misunderstanding ; that, after all, there was no cause for such an awful quarrel, and that the honor of both parties could be preserved without a resort to arms.

"I have hope, though, yet ; for gentlemen have been known, when they arrived upon the ground to settle their private quarrels, attended in silence by friends and surgeons, in the coldest and grayest dawn of the morning, to listen, when the stillness preceding the conflict had become so deathly that they could hear well, to suggestions of the above description. I humbly pray it may be so with the impending quarrel of our country ; else these times are sadly out of joint. I am deter-

mined to do all I can, when the time comes, to
make people listen to reason; and if all, both North
and South, who think as I do, would only act, the
trouble would be avoided."

"May 8.

" I was delighted to receive your letters, and
think their sentiments are truly patriotic. I love
my country, and shall try to serve it in this its
hour of need, which is not to be done in this State
without great prudence and greater sacrifices; but
between a mal-administration of a government the
best in the world and the chances of none at all, I
have deliberately chosen, upon the 'Hamlet Un-
discovered' principle, in favor of the former.

" I hope the President and his co-workers in
power will be quiet with their Missouri army for
a time at least, for we are stronger without them
than with them, and have need of all our strength.
Affairs are not pleasant in this State. The present
picture, turn which way you will, is fearful to look
upon, and still more so to contemplate for the
future. It requires some physical and moral courage to travel through the towns and country at
the present time, and a barrier has been placed
in society in St. Louis which no one can pass. I
am called an abolitionist by people here in the
country, between whom and myself there has been

heretofore the highest mutual respect. I don't like all this, but cannot help it, and think, with a worthy Carondelet alderman, 'that the best thing what one can do is to do the best thing what one can.'

. . . .

" I have received your present, which gives me much pleasure. I return you my love, which now is all I can safely call my own ; but in sending you this gift do not fear that I am robbing myself, for this possession, among its other virtues, is in no danger of suffering by division or a modern secession."

To his mother, under date of June 1, he writes:

" In whatever light we view the present troubles of our country, it is a very serious affair, and the question must arise, whether the remedy used is not as bad as the disease to be cured. Civil war is a long and dreadful thing, and I have feared this for years. You of Massachusetts, who are one people, and sustained each by the sentiments of the other, do not and cannot realize what war is in a community divided against itself, where the partisan feeling enters society and erects barriers between friends, neighbors, inmates of the same house, and members of the same family. Evil

times have fallen upon us indeed, when that barrier widens from coolness to passion and from passion to arms. Yet such is the case here. In St.
Louis a line is drawn through society, and across
the barrier no social intercourse is allowed. Persons intimately connected with each other have
met in arms.

"I have taken my position for the Union, and as
a consequence for the government; for between a
good government badly administered and the un-
certainty attendant on forming a new one upon its
dismemberment, I could not hesitate to choose.
My position, therefore, in common with that of
many others, is one that requires prudence as well
as principle, and may involve much sacrifice.

"I have been pleased to see the promptness
with which my native State, stimulated by patriotism, has responded to the call of her government
believed to be in danger, and I am pleased with
the whole North, which volunteers to sustain the
rightful authority of law. The supremacy of law
as such, whether believed to be just or unjust, is
the only safeguard of life, liberty, and property,
and all differences should be adjusted under the
law, until oppression marks the time to take up the
sword.

"I cannot forget, however, that the good people

of Massachusetts and other New England States
did not display upon the call of former executives
the same willingness to rush to arms in wars with
foreign powers, one of which was for defending
the rights of their own commerce and seamen, as
they now display in a war, at best, to chasten the
errors of their brethren; and I hope, if Providence designs by these troubles lessons of wisdom,
that it may be a part of that divine plan to distrib-
ute a small number among the people of the North.
The North cannot be held entirely guiltless in this
fearful, awful war."

From Journal, June 5 : —

" Have been to St. Louis: stopped at my old
home, and found W—— had a French consul house-
keeping with him. I found also that extremely
bitter hostility is felt towards the government in
the aristocratic circles, which enters into every
relation, both business and social. I feel utterly
incapable, at times, to understand this feeling ;
and I also feel sometimes that I would fly from
the bitter cup before me.

" Here are men — 'near a whole city full' —
who have heretofore gloried in our government,
and served it faithfully, some of them, — can they

be disloyal now? There are men here who have proved themselves sound in judgment in everything pertaining to the political economy of our country, men that I honor, love, and revere, men that would not flinch from any sacrifice, — can they be misguided now?

"I am overwhelmed by these reflections at times; but I must be just and honest with myself in this matter, cost what it will."

There is a pause here of some weeks; the pen makes no record either by letter or journal; the curtain is suffered to drop over the inner conflict still going on; no ear heard, no eye saw, save that which neither slumbers nor sleeps. But the following letter, bearing date July 15, gives proof that his heart was now at rest; that he had espoused openly the Union cause, although he had not then decided to take up arms in defence of his country.

"JEFFERSON CITY, July 15.

"DEAR S——: I am rain-bound here to-day, with thin and soiled garments; it is cold and disagreeable. It rains nearly all the time now-a-days, and I expect the storm of to-day will entirely ruin my wheat, which has been a long time in the field, and ought to have been thrashed long ago; for

you must know, my dear S——, that I have par-
taken of the belligerent spirit of the times, and
am determined to thrash that wheat. For this
purpose I have made every preparation, — have
put all my implements of war into the field, have
raised men and horsemen, — and the first fair day
I shall make the attack.

"My infantry will make the first charge. This
manœuvre will throw the enemy into such a position that, by a vigorous movement of the cavalry,
I will knock all their heads off; and by continuing
hostilities in this manner I hope to show that my
enemy is a mere man of straw.

"After I get my adversary into my own power,
tightly imprisoned, I shall carry him away and
sink him in a dark dungeon, and mash him, which
I think will completely subjugate him; unless at
some future time, perhaps when peace and plenty
shall smile again, and we all are happy around
the social board, trusting to the careless security
of the times, and instigated by yeast, he shall rise
again. But if that event should occur, I am determined to eat him.

"My dear sister, you will think I am carrying
the simile rather too far; but you cannot judge of
war in your peaceful home. There are reckless,
foolish men around me, and all over the State, who

18

are continually exasperating the opposite party,
creating everywhere a petty civil war. There
have been fatal fights within a few miles of me,
in every direction; but so far, by common consent,
we preserve amity and good neighborhood. I have
tried every honorable means to maintain this state
of things, and feel grateful for my success so far,
as I am an avowed Union man. Such sentiments
are not always to be expressed with safety. I tell
all Union men who wish to take an active part
in this contest to join the army; secessionists
the same; for the formation of home guards in
this State is bad policy. I appeal to the selfish
interests of all for industry, which is so necessary to both the soldier and the citizen, that it
may not perish entirely throughout the State, as
well as that the barbarities of such a strife may
be prevented as far as possible. Our State is in
a terrible condition, and it will be a long time
before it recovers from it.

"Last night I received your letter, and will tell
you, as near as can be told, what I am doing. I
am 'existing;' this is about all. I feel that my
country is in trouble, and that it is a time when
men, if they are needed, should not merely look
on : and this feeling makes me uneasy, for the
reason that my business connections are yet so

elaborate and unsettled that there seems to be a necessity laid upon me to attend to them, — a necessity imposed upon me as much by obligations to others as myself. There are so many people here to whom I furnish employment in my mills, and on the farm, in clearing up new ground in the vicinity, — some mainly for the reason that it is their only means of obtaining the necessaries of life, — that in this I find a pleasant occupation.

"As for society, I have none, and feel little desire for any. Everything is so unsettled, and the times are so stirring and eventful, that to keep one's self fully informed leaves little time for other reading or study."

From journal: —

"CASTLE ROCK, August 11, 1861.

"I went into Jefferson City this afternoon, and while there reports came of the death of General Lyon. It seems but a day since I met him here on his way to Springfield, and had such satisfactory converse with him. How often my mind has reverted to his pure, honest, sincere character, and the hopes it gave me in the service of his country; and now he has fallen! A feeling of sadness at the loss of this heroic general has oppressed me beyond measure.

"In addition to this sad event, news reaches me of the death of C—— G——. This brings to my mind a long train of memories, which the recollection of mutual association brings back from the past. A sorrowful picture of the horrors of war! The accounts of this battle, and the results it leaves, have begotten in me a feeling of personal responsibility, which leads to serious consideration.

"The action of the government seems inadequate to the necessities of the State, and the Union men here seem to rely too much upon the government to do, at least in part, their own work. I apprehend that Jackson and the Confederate forces will soon appear in large numbers at some point near the interior of the State, and that the friends of the rebellion, more ready than the friends of the country, will join them in large numbers. Shall Union men look on? Will it be all that we can do to listen for the news? I believe now is the time when my country, my native land, needs me and my all, and that here is the place.

"What can I do? Just now words or votes or civil government cannot do much. The appeal is to arms, and in arms must be met. I see but two ways, — to take arms or look on. I have no family; am young; business considerations should not weigh. I cannot be of service as a private soldier, or even as a company officer. Physical disease and exposure have unfitted me to endure what would be necessary, and at the time needed, in those positions, I fear I should fail. Am I fit. ted for a higher position? Could I fill it in such a manner as to make the forces I should command an absolute additional force? Could I obtain such a position?

"On my way home I sketched in my mind the scheme of raising a battalion of three companies, to volunteer for one year, as aid in suppressing the rebellion in Missouri. This is the State of my adoption and my love. My heart is here, my home is here, and the government of my fathers is mine. I must do something; and I ask the first of these questions intending to search myself in good faith; the second I shall set about solving to-morrow; and by the day following I will try to decide."

The following letter to his mother will show the result of the foregoing reflections : —

"CASTLE ROCK, August 14.

"DEAR MOTHER: I am just home from Jefferson City, twelve o'clock at night. I was detained late by business, and came very near being detained all night by the picket guard, as Jefferson City is now under martial law.

18*

"The war news you see by the daily press; I will not speak of it in general terms, but enclose you a paper showing what I intend to do. I have considered this step more seriously than any act of my life, and am firmly convinced that it is my duty. I hope that you and my father will approve it.

"I have strenuously opposed that party which have unnecessarily aggravated the causes of this war; but that reckless men have hurried the war upon us does not obviate the fact that it is here, and that good men must take firm, positive ground. I love my country, and cannot consent to let it go without my effort.

"Pardon a short letter, as I have a great deal of writing to do, and to-morrow I go to Linn, to address a meeting of our county. I am well, in good spirits, and love my father and mother as well as ever.

"Your affectionate son,
"GEO. B. BOOMER."

It would be impossible to describe the sufferings, the discouragements, the difficulties of such a stand as this brave young man took, — that he would take up arms in defence of his country, — and the almost insurmountable obstacles in the way of raising a regiment in such a disloyal atmosphere.

It is an easy matter to talk of acting from purely conscientious motives; it is no hardship to say that we will judge of things from their intrinsic merits, and that we will act independently, as those who must give account unto God. This is the theory, which if developed into action makes moral heroes in any and every sphere in life, whether they be kings or peasants, living in the city or country, laboring on the battle-field or in the humble shop. But it is not so easy to stand unmoved and fixed in the truth in the presence of adversaries. Human nature is weak; it loves approbation; and it is much more congenial for the heart to glide easily down the stream of popular sentiment than to buffet against the tide. It is hard to stand by one's principles, to be true to one's self, when on every hand, in looks, in words, in conduct, we meet with opposition, with coldness, yea, with almost hatred. We are linked to our fellow-men by so many unseen but beautiful threads of sympathy, that when we feel that support to be gone, and we walk almost solitarily and alone for truth's sake, — suffer trial and persecution for its maintenance, — the reason and judgment are very apt to find some ground, in the pressure of circumstances around us, for escaping so severe an ordeal.

It is easy to be generous in deed, magnanimous in action, heroic and self-sacrificing in life, when our ears are filled with public applause, when our hearts beat quickly with the approving smile and the meed of love, when by such acts we see friends increase, and our position in the community greatly dignified thereby. But when there is no eye to see except to look coldly, when there is no ear to hear except to condemn, when there is no hope except in firm reliance upon principle, then comes ofttimes the night of weeping, the heart-searching, the inner voice uplifted to that Eye which is never shut, that Ear which is never closed.

But such training, although severe, often forms the noblest characters, and gives them a calm, un-shrinking confidence in the cause they espouse. They may be weighed down by difficulties, op-pressed by fears, but having thus triumphed over self, having fought this first great battle victori-ously, there is little fear of faltering.

The most brave, heroic act of Mr. Boomer's life was not in shedding his blood before the strong-hold of Vicksburg, although on that sad evening the setting sun cast its lingering rays upon the pale brow of as true and loving a patriot as was

ever graced by the "white plume of Navarre;"
but it was while toiling for months in raising his
regiment, poor and almost unfriended, that he displayed a courage and endurance more grand than
the hottest fight of any battle-field could have
offered. In the excitement of action the soldier
is stimulated by the circumstance of war, by martial harmonies, by the immediate hope of success,
by many motives kindred to those around; he is
sustained by a mighty host, a strength he be-
lieves invincible; he is impelled to deeds of dar-
ing which make the "world wonder," while at the
same time they pronounce him a hero; but it is
not so sublime, so pure, so lofty a heroism as that
which is displayed by him who works for his
country without the aid of sympathy or remu-
neration.

The men of loyal hearts in Missouri at this period were a small band of patriots, so small and
so widely scattered that each seemed as it were
standing alone. But their patriotism was not a
covering of blue and gold, to be put on for ambition or display; it was a patriotism that had
passed through the furnace, and bore the test of
purity. It was a patriotism that could bear "the
crack of prowling rifles," that could look upon
burning homes, murdered fathers, houseless wives,

and fatherless children. The sufferings of the
people of Missouri can never be told. They were
accustomed to pass sleepless nights and perilous
days, to see property in every form stolen. The
Union and Confederate armies had both passed
through the State, which, combined with the bitter hatred and enmity of its inhabitants, made it
one scene of devastation and ruin.

It was at such a time as this that Mr. Boomer
undertook to raise a thousand men to fight in the
defence of our country; and with such feelings as
the following passage indicates he commenced the
work : —

"I know that in taking this step many, I fear
most of those I have best loved for years, will
condemn and forsake me. In the dear city of my
love my name will be spoken of as evil, and every
plan of my life I yield. My family are too far away
to give me the support I need, and which it would
be their pleasure to bestow; but I cannot and
would not do otherwise than I have done. The
struggle is over, and I feel sure of success."

A friend at Castle Rock says : —

"Mr. Boomer had frequent conversations with
me at the commencement of the war in regard to

his own duty, in the then distracted state of the country, and upon mature reflection he decided to raise a regiment. No sooner had he come to this decision than he promptly set about the work with all his known energy, and from motives of pure patriotism."

Another friend says : —

" How Mr. Boomer was to raise a regiment in our poor, disloyal country, was a mystery, and how he was to leave his large business interests and prepare himself for a military commander, was equally unaccountable. But he was a man, although young, who had the confidence of all who knew him, was beloved by all classes, and had that popularity which would insure his success if any one, under the unfavorable circumstances, could succeed.

" He first established his camp at Castle Rock, freely giving to the soldiers the use of his household furniture, his beds, bedding, table furniture, and everything he had which would add to their comfort. After a few weeks he changed his quarters to Medora, where he at the same time could give his personal attention to military discipline."

He had great difficulty in turning the minds of
the people to right views of maintaining the government, and to aid in accomplishing this he
travelled from town to town, addressing the people, urging their loyalty, and many, says a friend,
out of love to him joined his regiment. Sometimes days would pass without any apparent progress, and he would be told by his friends that he
never could succeed; but he heeded not such
prophecies, only to put forth greater effort. There
was a power in his soul which lifted him above the
fear of defeat; amidst the ravings of the storm
around he was calm and unshaken. "As anchored
ships cling to rifted rocks amid howling tempests,
so he clung to the truth," believing in its power to
sustain.

There was but one thing which he counted a
sacrifice, one grief, and that was the loss of his
friends. On this subject he was usually silent, but
an occasional remark told the depth of his feelings.

One evening, when sitting in a concert-room at
St. Louis, some of his dear old friends came in and
stood near him. He looked at them very earnestly
and tenderly; then, turning to the friend sitting
by his side, he said, "God only knows what this
has cost me. This is a test which you of the
Northern States can never know."

Worn down by constant fatigue, he went from town to town, from county to county, and in an easy, simple, friendly manner, urged the people to loyalty; as may be seen by the following memoranda of meeting with the people of Linn County :

" I am glad, fellow-citizens, to see you here, so many of you, to testify, by your presence at least, your concern for the public good.

" What is there so noble, so touching, in all the spectacles humanity presents, as the stirring of that impulse of the human heart which leaps to the rescue of distress? When we see it in the individual it melts our hearts into sympathy. It is this divine instinct which impels the mother to leap to the rescue of her child, regardless of her own peril, and our hearts glow with admiration for that mother. But when we see the rushing of a mighty people to the rescue of their common country in distress, when we see them willing to imperil all they have to sustain that government which bears within it the seeds of happiness and the tree of liberty, what shall we call that impulse but an approach to the higher nature of which man is said to bear the germ?

" Has the world ever seen the like of that spectacle which, four months ago, it beheld in the loyal

19

people of this country, responding to the call of the President to save the nation from the foe that attacked it? Was it the less sublime that the foe was within its own borders, and that, with a sense of their own loyalty to deceive them, they had hugged the sweet dream of peace and concession until the treacherous enemy had nearly encompassed them in their destructive folds? No! rather the more sublime! And I am glad indeed to believe, fellow-citizens, that you, or most of you, partook of this disinterested sentiment of loyalty, and that you are here by your presence to testify thereto.

"But while the impulses of the heart are noble, yet, as related to great actions, they should be tempered by judgment and intelligence; and I am here to consider the principles which I have embodied in the following resolutions: —

"*Resolved*, That we have a country which we love from patriotism; that we have a government which we love for its intrinsic worth, and the blessings it has conferred upon us; that we have a flag which we love from all the memories that cluster around it; that as American citizens all these are ours; and that we will defend them from the most dangerous of internal foes.

"*Resolved*, That a minority of the people, de-

ceived by ambitious men, without cause (except
evil passions) have rebelled in arms against the
peaceful will of the majority ; that they have done
violence to our Constitution and the peaceful customs of our whole history ; and that as we love
peace, as we love liberty, as we love our domestic happiness, and as we hope to secure obedience
to all constituted authority hereafter, it is the duty
of the government to put this rebellion down, and
our own duty to aid in doing the same.

"*Resolved,* That as citizens of Missouri we are
also citizens of the United States, and that no government can be said to invade its own citizens ;
that as citizens in our own state capacity we have
been outraged by a conspiracy on the part of our
former executive and legislative officers, against
our honor, our interests, and our sovereign will as
expressed in convention, and that, led by these
men, our homes are invaded and our property
stolen ; that our convention in secret session has
done its duty in deposing those men who violated
our rights, and in providing us new officers, and
that we will sustain its action, — obey the call of the
authorities to compel the peace and drive the in-
vaders from our soil ; that the cry of our enemies
for peace is a call for us to surrender our rights in
law, liberty, and native land ; that these are inalien-

able, and guaranteed to us by our Constitution, and
that we will never surrender them; but that we
will call upon *them* for peace, — that they restrain
their madness by laying down their arms, and obey
the laws, enjoy their protection, and take again
their equal share in the glories and blessings of
our common land."

A few extracts from letters give some indications that he had difficulties to overcome in preparing for his new sphere of life : —

"September 11, 1861.

"DEAR S——: I can write you but a few words
to-night, as I am very busy forming my regiment,
and getting my business and property into such a
condition that it can be safely attended to during
my absence, or disposed of should I never return.
It is a great deal of trouble to do both. The military affairs at St. Louis are very imperfectly
managed, which, in the confusion created heretofore, and partially now, from want of proper state
authorities, makes additional trouble. I am making as much progress, considering these things, as
could reasonably be expected, and am fully satisfied
that I am doing what I should do.

"I am thankful for your letters, and feel happy

when I know that those I love still care for me, and it will aid me.

"Raising a regiment in this State is attended with much difficulty, and I may be disappointed, but perseverance and tact will accomplish much. It is right to serve my country, and I must 'crown my thoughts with acts.' I am gratified with the feeling that I have been the cause of inducing many men to go into the field who otherwise would not have done so.

"Give love to A—— and the children, and reserve for yourself on the unfailing principle of the widow's cruse."

"November 2.

"What can I say to you in detail, my dear sister? I do not like to deny what you ask me, but sometimes it is best I should.

"My regiment is still at Medora, recruiting very slowly, but with a good prospect for the coming week, and I hope in a short time to be full.

"I have seen our new major-general in command of the State, and could not be better pleased, so far as appearances go. I think he is quite perplexed by the situation here, and scarcely knows what to do, which I do not wonder at; in fact, it will hardly be expected that he will be able to take intelligent action for some days.

19*

" As soon as my regiment is full I want to go to Benton barracks and get thoroughly prepared for the field, and then go south. I would like to visit New Orleans with an escort.

" My dear sister, why do you beg to know all the particulars of what I am doing, thinking, etc.? The daily events of my life would only fill your heart, already anxious enough, with more solicitude. These are hard times for Union men in Missouri; but I am a man, my good sister. You always had a little comfort in such reflections about me, — at least you have sometimes flattered me in that way, — and now I have an opportunity of ' testing my metal.' "

"November 18, 1861.

" DEAR S——: I am as busy as I can be, drilling, holding school, etc. My duties begin at early dawn and last until eight o'clock P. M.

" My regiment is likely to be affected by General Halleck's policy, as he stopped further recruiting some time ago, turned it over to the State forces, and is going to consolidate all regiments not full. I may lose my position by this arrangement, but I will not fail to do my duty in any event. I have great faith in General Halleck, and if I have to suffer it will be the result of a policy which I think he ought to adopt under all circumstances.

"I more than appreciate your kindness, and it greatly aids me. I cannot say more, only to beg that you will not distress yourself about me, for you know, my sister, — I have often heard you say it, — that 'it is a noble thing to suffer and be strong.' I have made up my mind to do what I am doing for a cause I love, and though new and worse difficulties should arise, I shall not turn back. I am happy in this, never more so."

CHAPTER XII.

THE SOLDIER.

—— " To fight
In a just cause and for our country's glory
Is the best office of the best of men."

THE following letter will show that Mr. Boomer had accomplished his work of raising a regiment : —

" St. Louis, January 11, 1862.

" DEAR SISTER: I need not say that I was very thankful for your last kind letter, — except that the acknowledgment is becoming in me, — and I hope you will continue to write me often, even though I should seem unmindful of a proper return. Your letters always give me pleasure ; a fresh breathing comes with them through the air, and I respire for a while lighter and freer. The world of affection is one of its own, and when we enter it truly we have stepped out for the moment from the world of care as perfectly as in sleep, which the poets have always contended 'hath its own world.'

"I am at the Planters' House, writing after tea in the sitting-room, and the crowd buzzes about as it only can at an American hotel. Sunday, at the proper loafing hour, it reaches its climax, and this is I think the hour; in other words, 'the hour and the men are come.'

"I am expecting Mr. V—— B—— and my assistant surgeon on the train shortly. I sent for them, as to-morrow morning it is proposed to muster into the service the whole field and staff of the Twenty-sixth Regiment Missouri Volunteers,— George B. Boomer, Colonel; John H. Holman, Lieutenant-Colonel; L. H. Koninszesky, Major; Dr. Prout, Surgeon; Dr. Bryan, Assistant Surgeon; A. H. Van Buren, Adjutant: chaplain and quartermaster I have not yet appointed.

"The forces under my command were consolidated, December 30th, with those of the lieutenant-colonel and major, and my position is the more flattering as it was given without my knowledge.

"I believe I am to be placed at Franklin, the junction of the Pacific and Southwest Branch Railroad, thirty-seven miles from here. I cannot, of course, tell what will ultimately be our destination, but I hope south. I have entered the service for

war, and, after due preparation, want to be where
the hardest work is to be done."

In entering the field Colonel Boomer assured his
friends that it would be vain for them to look for
a labored correspondence from him; that he should
have neither time nor disposition to write a history of the movements of the army as they occurred. He should enter the field for work, and if
he attended faithfully to his duties it would leave
him neither time nor thought for digesting or
condensing the active operations of a large body
of soldiers for newspaper correspondence. This
opinion was fully confirmed, after a little observation in the field, by seeing the personal aims
and ends of the press, many of them utterly false,
or at least with truth so distorted that it was
hard to recognize it even as a foundation.

The Twenty-sixth Missouri remained in the State
service as guard until the sixteenth of February,
when they were ordered to Fort Donnelson; but
as our army was victorious at that place before
they could reach it, they were ordered to Bird's
Point, from there to Charlestown, Missouri, and
thence to Bertrand and New Madrid.

From the latter place Colonel Boomer wrote a
letter showing that he fully appreciated the dan-

gers to which a soldier was exposed on the field of battle : —

"CAMP NEAR NEW MADRID, March 13, 1862.

"DEAR SISTER : I write you a hurried note this eve, as we are ordered to be ready for an advance to-morrow by daylight.

"I have seen hard times of late, as we marched thirty-eight miles in two days to get here, without tents or baggage, or scarcely anything to eat. We did not have our horses, so I marched with the soldiers, sleeping on the ground one night in the rain, which was too much for me, as I have not recovered my strength from the illness I had at Bird's Point.

"I do not know what we shall do to-morrow, but I hear heavy firing to-night, proceeding, I think, from the enemy's gunboats upon our batteries below, on the river.

"We have a superior force, but the enemy has great advantage in position. I judge that the present intention is to advance on the lines ; but whatever is done, or commanded to be done, I believe I shall be able to do my duty.

"I am in General Schuyler Hamilton's division, whom I know well. We are friends, and I feel sure that I shall be fairly treated, and well cared for if wounded.

"I send you a bill of sale of my library and household furniture, which I want you to have in case accident happens to me.

"L—— was to see me at Bertrand. We had a good brotherly visit. He was full of kindness, and we parted as I marched for this place. May Heaven bless him for all his love to me.

"Please transmit the contents of this letter to my mother, L——, and N——, with my love to you *all*. I can only write to mother my love, and tell her she will hear through you.

"With much love to your husband, to Ara and Bella,
        "I am ever your dear brother,
                        "George."

            "Hamburg, Tennessee, April 23, 1862.

"Dear S——: After the siege of New Madrid we crossed the river at Tiptonville. We were present at the surrender of Island No. 10, went down to Fort Pillow with the fleet, and while there received orders to move to this place immediately.

"I am quite happy in my position; yet I assure you I would be glad to get out of it were it not for the object with which I entered the service. It is a hard, thankless life; save the idea that it is necessary, one could not endure the horrors of war. It has its sunlights, however, and I shall be happy in the experience of this self-denial, should I be so fortunate as to survive it. My health is excellent, and I feel confident that my regiment will do well.

"I beg you will excuse a short letter, for it is the first time for more than a week that we have had any ink or stationery, and consequently I have an accumulation of writing on my hands.

"We have been in slow pursuit of the flying enemy since the 30th, and succeed in keeping just about so near him, having nothing but blankets and ammunition with us, saving very little to eat.

"I believe now we shall stop and occupy the railroads and the country through which we pass, which, after so long a time, is the most sensible thing we can do.

"I am generally well, and am at present in command of a demi-brigade, three regiments, — Fifth Iowa, Fifty-seventh Indiana, and my own. I commanded them before Corinth, and had the honor to lead them into one little skirmish which was quite brilliant."

On going into the field Colonel Boomer was presented with a very fine horse. The generous donor had spared no pains in the training of this noble animal, and during the seige of Corinth it

20

won the reputation of being the finest animal in the field: but most unfortunately its fame extended to the rebel camp. Colonel Boomer, in the foregoing letter, says: " I have lost my fine horse. I loaned him to my chaplain one day, when riding, to go back on the road to see a sick officer; returning, he strayed a little from the road, and was captured by the enemy. The chaplain I have heard from, — he is in good hands, — but there still remains an uncomfortable silence about the horse."

The sequel of the stolen horse was afterwards revealed. While at Corinth one of the rebel generals had his eye upon this horse, with the determination to capture it. This he succeeded in doing, as about six months afterward he sent a note of thanks to the Colonel for his splendid animal.

                               " IN THE FIELD, July 7, 1862.

" DEAR S——: Your kind letters from home reached me in due time, and they are so welcome that I dare not let this last one go by without a reply, for fear I may miss them hereafter if I neglect you. This is very selfish, is it not? but you know it is the mainspring of many of our acts. Still, I have another reason, for you know that I love to write you. So here goes.

" First, the situation, — a block for a seat, a

tent-fly for a roof, a field desk and a candle: the air, the open field, constitute my other surroundings.

"It is a warm, moonlight evening; tattoo has been beating an hour; the horses are grazing, picketed; and there is systematic outbreak of noise among the mules and wagons, and a hum, low but distinct, along the stacks of arms stretched along this road, which runs east and west from Rienzi to Jacinto. I am in this open field on the south side of the road, the men and the arms on the north, and we are all two miles east of Rienzi, 'whither two horsemen may frequently be seen riding.'

"We have been marching, without tents or baggage, ever since June 26th, east and west, for about fifty miles, along this road, to near Holly Springs, an average distance of twenty miles south of Corinth. The enemy are hovering about, but I think only in small force, without any other motive than to annoy us.

"I feel often heartsick at what I see about me, which, with all the privations and the 'often infirmities' of the temporal man, very frequently make hard times. But the more I see of the strength of our foe in this part of the country, combined with our recent disasters East, the more

I feel that this gigantic war is by no means over; and as I entered the service for three years or the war, I have not the least idea of leaving it, so long as I may be of use in accomplishing the great end.

"I would like to see home and you, and I would like many other things; but I counted all these privations in the cost of being a soldier, and have no expectation of leaving the army while there is any use in my being in it, except when required to do so by serious wounds or illness. I do not believe in so many officers leaving the army on furloughs; it demoralizes and disorganizes everything. I know it is pleasant to rest, but if war is a necessity let us meet it as a necessity."

"August 1.

"Do not worry too much about me, my sister. It is true that we often have hard times, that we sometimes get desponding, but there is much to enjoy, aside from the fact that we are laboring for a country which has need of us. We come in contact with the brightest intellects in the land. These intellects, sharpened by action, called out by corresponding minds, bound together by a common sympathy, afford no inferior enjoyment. And then life is so active, so intense, so much is crowded into a single day or hour."

" My regiment has gone to Jacinto, twelve miles southwest of here. I shall join them to-morrow if as well as to-day.

" As I write I hear the guns of the batteries of the First Missouri Light Artillery, including Totter's and Dubois's. They are saluting the anniversary of the battle of Willson's Creek. I now hear the guns of the Second Kansas; they claim their honors too. This interests me, as that battle decided me to enter the army.

" I am truly thankful for your letters ; they are better than an oasis, for, as I travel along the desert, I can carry the fountain and shade with me.

" I rejoice that you are with our dear parents again, and wish I could ride with you to our old home in Sutton. The older I grow the more vivid is my childhood. Remember me to all my acquaintances of those early years, as you see them.

" With love to all,

" I am your affectionate brother,

" GEORGE."

" CAMP AT JACINTO, August 13.

" DEAR SISTER N——: I came to this place yesterday, where my regiment have been for several days. I found your letter to welcome me, which

was a real happiness, — greater than I can tell.
How delightful to hear that you are in better
health. I believe you will permanently recover.
As a family we all have great vitality, and since I
have been in the service I have borne the hard-
ships well.

" The weather is very warm, but I dread more
a certain quality of heat than I do the quantity.
There are some peculiar properties of heat that
reduce one.

"Altogether I like the service, and get on much
better than I feared, though, like everything else,
there are many trials connected with it.

" You speak of my life. It has been much as
you think, and from year to year I feel more
strength and purpose. I shall never be too old or
too wise to learn, and so day by day I receive a
new pleasure. ' Whom the Lord loveth he chas-
teneth.' I have sometimes thought those words
were meant for me; they are beautiful, and have
given me much comfort.

"You say that Johnny wants to be a soldier.
He is too young to enter the army. No one has a
right, except as a last resort, to enter the field
until his physical development is complete. To
do so brings ruin upon his future, and does little
or no present good. A more rigid inspection,

throwing out nearly twenty per cent. of the re-
cruits, would save millions of dollars, and give us
a stronger army."

A few weeks after the foregoing letter was
written, our troops were engaged in the battle of
Iuka. This contest demanded prompt and energetic action, which was met by Colonel Boomer
with a determination to conquer, as will best be
seen by the following account of the battle, taken
from the public press : —

" In this engagement seven or eight thousand
of our troops fought against eighteen to twenty
thousand of the enemy. The nature of the ground
was such, also, that they could approach very near
us without being exposed.

" Our battery took its position on a point where
two ridges join. On each is a road, both converg-
ing at this place. The line of the First Brigade
formed nearly at right angles with the battery on
the point of the angle.

" The enemy poured grape and shell upon our
troops all the time they were forming, and charged
almost before our line was completed.

" When our battery opened, as it did, double
charged with ammunition, it made fearful havoc in

the enemy's deep columns; but still they came
upon us, with such a concentrated fire, that the
battery was silenced, and the three regiments on
the left gave way.

"Meantime Colonel Boomer, of the Twenty-sixth
Missouri, seeing the danger, and that the battery
was gone, moved his regiment forward, and by the
off flank on and around the battery, fought against
both a front and flank fire with the most unparal-
leled determination, sustained by the Fifth Iowa.
During the fearful struggle Colonel Boomer had
no field or staff officer to assist him; yet he was
everywhere seen in the fight, apparently at the
same time. Three times had he to rally his brave
men to this deadly contest, one-half of whom were
left on the battle-field, killed or wounded.

"In this hot fight the Colonel had received two
balls in his thigh. Still undaunted, he pressed
on, — no surrender with him, — until, as night
closed in, another ball threw him from his horse,
as it was supposed mortally wounded, but not
until he had the satisfaction of knowing that the
victory was ours, which victory justly covered him
with glory."

For some days Colonel Boomer's wounds were
considered mortal. In contemplating death he ex-

pressed an entire trust in the all-wise Disposer of events, and said if it was God's will that he should end his earthly career at that time he was satisfied, and knew that he should not be left to tread "the dark valley" alone. One of his friends expressed her grief that he had thus sacrificed his life. He said reprovingly, "And you call this sacrifice, if I lose my life or become disabled? It is a price to be paid, but not too dear for the blessings of a good government. I would not have my country go through such a struggle without feeling the satisfaction that I had, in thought and in act, given it my entire, my most hearty sympathy. Our nationality must be maintained."

During this illness he was asked if he thought the war was nearly at an end. He replied that he thought not. He believed that certain successful campaigns on our part, such as taking their largest cities and their strongholds, might bring the hardest fighting to an end; but even that was going to be a difficult thing to do, and in that event the South would resist us by every means in their power. He was convinced the South would never lay down their arms and return to the Union so long as they had any ability to fight; and until their institutions were entirely changed, peace would never smile upon our land again, for "our

enemy was really fighting for aristocracy, and
their leaders were haughtier despots than were
ever enthroned by the most arbitrary laws in any
age."

While recovering from his wounds he was permitted to go north, and one circumstance after
another led him to pay a visit to every member
of his family. This privilege seemed to fill him
with a new happiness, and although not usually
demonstrative, yet he could not sufficiently express
his pleasure in seeing all his friends again. To
use his own words, "they all seemed invested
with a new interest to him." Perhaps the shadow
of this earthly farewell was hovering over him.

On returning to his command he stopped at St.
Louis, and, as if guided by an overruling hand, he
made a short visit to Castle Rock. Of his visit
to St. Louis he says : "I rejoice to be here once
more, and greatly rejoice in the more plentiful
number of Union people than when I left it. I am
surprised at the change of feeling towards me, as
my old friends very generally seem delighted to
greet me. It was reported here that I was killed,
and one of my good friends was on the point of
sending to Corinth for me, when it was ascertained
that my brother had already gone."

In speaking of this visit, a friend says: "Colonel

Boomer seemed quite astonished at the enthusiasm with which he was everywhere greeted in going up and down the road from Jefferson City to St. Louis, and at the former place. As for the people of Castle Rock, their joy was unbounded when they heard he was going to pay them a visit. He was expected there the day before he went, and all his friends were gathered to meet him. As the next day went by without his appearing, they began to fear they should be disappointed ; but when, late in the evening, it was announced that their dear Colonel was crossing the river, men, women and children rushed to the landing, and with one burst of joy gave him a welcome."

This visit to Missouri gave him great support and comfort, and on reaching his command, the 11th November, he says his life seemed full of blessings ; and, added to the joy of visiting old friends and sharing their confidence, his regiment received him in such a manner that he could not speak for some time.

Colonel Boomer was advised by many of his military friends to seize upon so favorable an opportunity to secure his promotion. The following letter will show the nature of his feelings upon this subject : —

OXFORD, MISSOURI, December 8.

" DEAR SISTER: Your kind letters are received; and let me thank you again for the interest you take in me, for it is rare, and I trust you believe that I bear no ungrateful heart towards you in return.

" I want to explain to you why I have taken no active measures to obtain promotion. I don't believe in it, and could not do it. Advancement is only valuable as it serves one's purpose. I have certain views of what is high and lofty in life, with which the means of advancement in these days do not always consort. I will not, in other words, do certain things to be promoted.

" My position is an honorable one, and one which gives me, in my own locality, all the reputation I deserve; for there is a true estimate of a man's qualities in the field; and if I am promoted it must be in such a way that I shall be proud of it, for it is not so distinguished an honor that great sacrifices should be made to attain it.

" I am fond of reflecting upon what I think have been right actions in my past career, that is, self-sacrificing and meritorious. I desire to enlarge this resource continually; and it is not to be done by advanced position, unless all other things are equal.

"Some things have occurred recently which afford me more satisfaction than any promotion the powers at Washington could give me without them. Shortly after I arrived here it was intimated that I was to be placed in command of a brigade, and when it was known that our division was to be reinforced with new regiments and reorganized, all the old regiments of the division, except two, applied to be assigned to my brigade.

"It would be egotistical for me to tell you of all the love and confidence that have been shown me in this affair, by men of all ranks; suffice to say, I feel really affected by it, and would not exchange it for forty brigadierships. General Grant has treated me with the utmost consideration. I had no right to expect it.

"I have been placed in command of General Schuyler Hamilton's old division at New Madrid, with the exception of the Fifty-ninth Indiana. It is composed of some of the very best regiments in the army; and I hope now to be of more use in subduing our foes than I have been heretofore."

This promotion in the army was followed by recommendations from Generals Grant, Rosecrans, Hamilton, Quimby, and others in the field, asserting that Colonel Boomer was an officer who had been tried, and deserved at the hands of his country the same promotion at Washington that had been given him unasked in the field. These recommendations were seconded by the governor and senators of Missouri; but at that time some favorite at Washington received the meed that was his due.

The following extracts from letters will show that Colonel B. felt deeply solicitous for our cause on return to the field: —

"January 8, 1863.

"DEAR S——: We are now on the Memphis and Charleston Railroad, fourteen miles from the city, guarding it. Our division guarded a train of five hundred wagons to Memphis and return, — the most disagreeable service we have had."

"January 19.

"We are going to Vicksburg as soon as we can get boats, — probably ten days yet. I am not over-cheerful in regard to matters in general."

Early in February he paid his last visit to St. Louis.

"CAMP NEAR MEMPHIS, February 22.

"MY DEAR SISTER: On my arrival here yesterday I found some late letters from you, and some old ones missing heretofore, covering a long interval, and bringing with them quite a retrospect. It seems, then, that I have at times written in blue lines. Well, that cannot be helped, for there are at times enough vexations to wear out the fortitude of the most patient of men. It is not at the necessary trials or obstacles to be overcome, but to see undone what might be done, and done what should not be done."

"GRAND LAKE LANDING, March 7.

"DEAR SISTER: We are one and a half miles north of Louisiana line, and twenty north of Lake Providence. It was intended to work through these lakes into Bayou Mascon, from thence into Red River, and through the latter into the Mississippi above Port Hudson. This plan is now abandoned, and we are going up the river to what is called the Yazoo Pass, on the Mississippi side. We expect to go through that pass into Moon Lake, thence into the Cold Water and Tallahatchie Rivers, and through these into Yazoo River, to a point above Vicksburg, which we propose to attack in the rear. There are five divisions going this route.

"I went yesterday down to Lake Providence to see General McPherson. It is one of the most

lovely spots in the world. The lake runs west
from the river, and is about three-fourths of a
mile wide. The water is clear, and skirted around
the edge of the shore with luxuriant trees, hung
with moss, so thick in places that it looks like a
veil. The banks are about twelve feet high. The
road runs along on the edge of it, which is lined
with elegant residences, the plantations running
back to the swamps. These plantations, deserted
by their owners, are now occupied by our troops;
while the generals in command find commodious
quarters in the fine houses.

"I wish you could see this wealth of beauty: it
is my first realization of the splendors of the Ori-
ental. The beautiful foliage and luxuriant flowers
and shrubs, profuse in fragrance, the brilliant birds,
gorgeous in coloring, combined with the freshness
of a sunny spring day, are enough to take one
away from the fact of a despoiling war into fairy
land.

"Well, there is always some sweet intermixed
with the bitter. Military matters do not look so
beautifully. I am not entirely pleased with the
present plan, and asked General McPherson to
go yesterday and see General Grant about it.
Whether he can effect any change remains to
be seen.

" General Grant is opposite Vicksburg, with half the army : the other half will be with us. I think they ought to be together. Whatever is done, the force should never be divided.

" I am well, and, though a good deal disquieted at times, I have made up my mind to see what I can do for my country. I will not entertain the idea of deserting what I have undertaken, but try to make the best of things as they are.

" I am so much obliged to you for your letters, and indeed I will write you more frequently than I have done : and if you will keep my letters I shall be glad. It might be a pleasure to me some time in the future to look them over and see what I thought and felt during this struggle, though they are poor affairs."

" HELENA. ARKANSAS. March 14.

" I am left here in charge of the Second and Third Brigades of this division, to procure transportation and embark them down the Yazoo Pass. General Quimby left this morning with the First Brigade."

" FLAG SHIP STEAMER W. W. CRAWFORD.
" AT LANDING, FIVE MILES BELOW HELENA.
" ARKANSAS. March 22. 1863.

" I have been waiting here a number of days for transports to take my command into Yazoo

21*

River. I have now obtained them, and we are embarked ready to leave to-morrow morning. We shall undoubtedly have a rough time of it working through a narrow, crooked bayou, overhung with trees, but we will work through nevertheless. The enemy will be likely to fight us too after we land, I think, as it will be their policy to do so before we get the rest of our forces in; but they will have a hard time at that, as we have good troops, consisting of eight regiments and three batteries.

"This expedition will prove a failure, I fear. My opinion has been expressed to General Grant and General McPherson in advance. I shall try my best, however, which is all the satisfaction from it that I look forward to. I am well and in good spirits."

"HEAD-QUARTERS STEAMER CRAWFORD,
"AT HELENA, April 11, 1863.

"DEAR SISTER: I waited for the aid of this bright morning to write you a cheerful letter.

"You remember that in Nursery Rhymes the King of France and Duke of York, with twice ten thousand men, did great things. We have done the same, under much greater difficulties, with half that number of men. We have demonstrated what can, and, more, what cannot be done. Well,

to come to the facts in the case, we have chased
the so-called Southern Confederacy up and down
all its small creeks, and I judge, from the effect our
movements have produced on ourselves, that we
have wrought very much confusion in the minds
of our enemies.

"I do not feel like making any review of my
expedition, even for your benefit, for I am in too
good humor. Still, you shall have some knowledge
of it, even from me.

"I will content myself now with saying, that,
after a trip which nearly worried the life out of
me, we arrived at Fort Greenwood. We remained
there two days and a half, which time I occupied
in reconnoitring, and talking to the enemy's pick-
ets,—the same enemy we met at Corinth and
Iuka, and who knew us at once, and were glad to
see us. At the expiration of this time, under
peremptory orders, we retired in good order, which,
under the circumstances, was quite surprising to
me, as the enemy saluted us with a few shells at
parting, and killed a few men by guerilla firing
from the banks. We arrived here last night, and
are going to Lake Providence to-day. Where our
future destination is, I don't know.

"Everybody feels disgraced, and the 'blue' is
the most prominent of the national colors of this

"On the trip down, while one morning in the pilot-house of the Belle Creole, a limb burst suddenly through, and cut my right eyelid badly.

"You would be amused to see our boats, — nothing but a photograph could describe them.

"My boat had to lie still about half the time, waiting for the others; and one day I gathered some beautiful flowers. I send you an apple blossom, which was most delicious when fresh, though there are few traces of its fragrance now."

"MILLIKIN'S BEND, April 20, 1863.

"DEAR S——: We are twenty miles above Vicksburg by water; arrived here the 15th.

"My brigade has a fine camp inside the levee along the river. General Grant's head-quarters are just on the right of my line.

"Colonel P—— is here, working nobly at a new canal, which will be a success for the object intended; viz., to supply our army below Vicksburg with provisions, etc. One *corps d'armée* (McClernand's) is already at Carthage.

"Eight gunboats and two steamboats ran the blockade Thursday night. It was the most magnificent sight I ever saw. Over five hundred shots were fired at them, which set fire to one of the steamers loaded with cotton. The rebels lighted a bonfire to illuminate the river; and between this and the flashes of the guns, the reports, and the explosion of the shells, together with the interest felt in the safety of the boats and crews, all conspired to create quite an excitement.

"Our prospects are brightening. The troops are concentrated, and can soon be used, I think."

"CAMP ON BIG BLACK RIVER, MISSISSIPPI, May 6.

"At last, through the 'many and various,' we are two days in bivouac as above.

"I am in excellent spirits. Major Brown is in here, and I am abusing him and having a real 'feast of reason' and 'flow of soul;' indeed, it is hard to bring myself down to write, being in a ripe condition to use my tongue instead of my pen; and while I know you are glad of it, yet I believe too you would like to have me make the sacrifice to write.

"I left Millikin's Bend the 25th April, and arrived here on the evening of May 3, having marched, by the route I took, about one hundred and twenty miles, a portion of the distance over horrible roads. I crossed my command over the Mississippi River in the interim, and laid by one day for other troops to pass, and moved the last day in the face of the enemy.

"Since General Grant commenced to move his columns he has displayed great tact and skill, together with immense energy and nerve. The passage of this army over the Mississippi River and up to this point is one of the most masterly movements known in the history of any warfare, and it is a success.

"We shall soon commence the second movement, when you will probably hear of a tremendous battle, and I trust a victory.

"You have no idea, my dear sister, of the beauty and wealth of this country. In Louisiana many of the plantations along the bayous and rivers are magnificent in the extreme, especially the grounds, covered with every variety of vegetation, all of the most luxuriant growth."

"Bivouac Five Miles East of Utica, on

"Raymond Road, Mississippi, May 12, 1863.

"Dear Sister: I am up very early this morning under orders to move, but am waiting for the columns to get off. It is about five o'clock A. M. I have had my breakfast; the air is damp, chilly and smoky. The dust, or something else, with a slight cold, have caused a soreness in my right lung and throat, so that I am feeling poorly.

"One thing which aids this condition is the news

in the Southern papers announcing another reverse to our arms in Virginia. I hope it may not be true, but the probabilities seem to be that it is. If so, there seems little hope of accomplishing anything there for a long time; and, besides, it will have a bad effect upon us here. We have enough before us at best, although the General is doing nobly, and has troops of great valor to bring him through.

"You will know by this time that I am not feeling well, and as I cannot send you a letter now, being in the Southern Confederacy, so called, I will await to-day's march."

"Sunday Evening, 17.

"Since I wrote the above I have seen and felt more than I can express to you.

"Our active operations began that day. We marched twelve miles, and fought a battle before Raymond. The forces engaged on either side were comparatively small, — one and a half divisions of ours, and about the same of the enemy.

"The night after the battle we bivouacked in Raymond. I led the advance toward Jackson; skirmished for eleven miles under dreadful heat and dust. The enemy did not engage his main force. I lost none; some were slightly wounded.

"The next morning (it rained all day) we met the enemy, under General Joe Johnson, eight miles in front of town. Our division joined in double line of battle, drove them from their position, captured their artillery, pushed them over their works and through the town, which we occupied at four o'clock P. M.

"The morning following we turned again for Vicksburg, made a march of sixteen miles, and yesterday, after marching five miles, met the enemy's whole army in splendid fashion, moved out to fight the battle of Vicksburg. We had but four divisions at hand to meet them with, and one of those could scarcely be said to have a part in the battle (Brigadier-General Osterhaus's). The other three were Hovey's, of McClernand's corps, General Logan's, and ours of McPherson's. General Grant and General McPherson were both on the field. General Logan's division and Sanborn's brigade were the right, General Hovey the left. I was ordered first left, then right, and finally, as the enemy massed all his force on General Hovey and commenced to rout him, I was ordered back again to the left, on the double quick, to support him. I did it manfully, though his force was completely routed by the time I got on the ground, and there was terrible danger of panic among my

men for a moment. As his scattered forces passed
by, I swung my lines into position under a terrible fire and drove them back. They reinforced
again and came up, at the same time endeavoring
to flank me on the left. I swung my left back
again, and held them until I received two regiments from Holmes's brigade, which enabled me to
drive them from the field.

"I captured what was left of a Georgia regiment and an Arkansas battalion. While we were
doing this, General McPherson had forced their
right, and they fled in utter consternation. The
result was the capture of two thousand prisoners
and sixteen pieces of artillery. The loss was
about equal on both sides.

"The great struggle was on the left. General
Hovey fought well; his men drove the enemy a
long distance; but they were all worn out, their
ammunition gone, and the enemy poured their
whole force against him.

"The victory was great and decisive, but, oh!
at how dear a cost to me! Five hundred and fifty-
one of my brave men were killed or wounded! I
cannot bear to think of it, — the way they fought
and fell.

"Major Brown, of my own regiment, is among
the killed. He was as noble and gallant as he was

pure and true, and his spirit will never die. He handled the regiment he commanded during that hot fight as though it were pastime, and his praise is on every tongue.

"Captain Welker was also killed, and we buried him, with Lieutenant-Colonel Horney of the Tenth Missouri and my dear friend Brown, this morning, side by side, in rude coffins, with a description of the locality, that will identify their graves if the rude mementoes we placed at their heads are lost.

"We are now at the crossing of the Big Black River, near the railroad crossing. A part of the enemy had not crossed when our forces reached here. General A. J. Smith's division, of McClernand's corps, charged on them, and they surrendered before our line reached them, — about three thousand in all.

"The enemy are totally demoralized, and a large force of them scattered in every direction. To-morrow we shall know what of Vicksburg. The indications are very favorable for us in every quarter of this campaign.

"I thank God that my life has been thus far spared, and trust it may be until the end. I have not been scratched. My horse yesterday was shot in the leg, but he kept the field with me. I think much credit is awarded me for my conduct, and I feel that I have done my duty.

"Our noble soldiers have borne every hardship, trial and fatigue, hunger, thirst, heat, and death, without a murmur."

CHAPTER XIII.

DEATH AND BURIAL.

HE last letter in the preceding chapter was received long after the hand that penned it lay cold in death.

The movements of our Western army, from its hour of triumph at Champion Hills (to which allusion is made in that letter) to the disastrous assault of the 22d of May upon the enemy's almost impregnable defences at Vicksburg, must be familiar to the mind of every reader.

On the morning of that day, General Grant issued an order that the whole line should make the assault at ten o'clock, a command that was promptly obeyed by Generals Sherman and McPherson; but this was not the case with General McClernand, who called for reinforcements before taking the field. In answer to General McClernand's request, the Seventh Division of General McPherson's corps was assigned him as a reinforcement; but, instead of its being kept as a reserve, it was ordered to the front.

It is maintained by many of Boomer's friends that from the moment this decision was known he looked apprehensively upon the result to himself, and said to one of them, standing near, that he should never see St. Louis again.

He was prostrated by the laborious campaign, fatigued by the fighting of the morning, disappointed at the result, and filled with a sense of injustice, that the worn troops should be sent to the front, while McClernand's fresh soldiers were kept in reserve. All these would naturally combine to fill his mind with depression, which might have been the only ground for belief that some foreshadowing of his fate rested upon him.

Before making that fatal charge he gave directions that in case he fell his body should be sent to his sister in Cleveland, Ohio; and remembering, with a tenderness peculiar to his nature, that dear home in Missouri, desiring in his last moments to recognize the tie that bound him to it, he also ordered that the field officers of his own regiment should bear his body from the battle-ground.

He then, with alacrity and cheerfulness, marched with his brigade to the scene of contest.

General Carr, in a private letter, says: —

" Boomer was perfectly cool and collected. He
22*

examined the position carefully, formed his men into two lines, took his place, and said, 'Boys, I shall be with you right between the lines,' and, giving the usual commands, marched them forward over the brow of and down the first hill or ridge.

"As soon as the men appeared over the brow of the ridge, the enemy's fire opened, and was terribly hot, but did not have much effect, as they fired high, and the men immediately commenced to descend the steep slope.

"At the bottom of this slope there was a ravine full of fallen trees and brush, very difficult to get over. After the men had scrambled across this, Boomer went on to the next ridge, and was making his arrangements for continuing his march, when he received his death wound.

" His last words were, 'Boys, don't charge those works.' He had discovered that it was too much for them to do."

This heroic officer was killed instantly by a bullet from the sharp-shooters, which pierced his head.

Whether he had any presentiment of his death or not, he had looked it in the face, and was prepared to meet it calmly as a condition of his loyalty, as a proof that he loved his country well.

There is a martyr's spirit in our war as true and grand as that which the poet comprehended, when, in describing the dying gladiator in the Roman arena, he painted him as one "whose manly brow consents to death, but conquers agony," a martyr's spirit more touching and sublime than any which "men or angels have ever gazed upon since they saw the drooping victim of Calvary's middle cross."

On learning the valuable service which this true-hearted patriot had accomplished for his country at Champion Hills, Governor Gamble again requested that the President should confer upon him the rank which had long been justly his due.

The following answer was received to this petition : —

"Gov. H. B. Gamble: In answer to your request, the President directs me to say that the government will testify its sense of the gallant conduct of Colonel Boomer by his appointment as Brigadier-General.

"Edwin M. Stanton,
"*Secretary of War.*"

In accordance with the wishes of this officer, the attempt was made to send his body north; but the facilities for embalming bodies were so imperfect in the army, and transportation was so difficult, that it was deemed advisable to bury him at Young's Point, until such time as his friends could furnish a safe passport.

A deputation was immediately sent from St. Louis to recover all that remained of him who had nobly made his last offering for his country; and on Sunday morning, June 21st, his body reached that city. It was conveyed at once to the Planters' House, where it lay in state until the funeral obsequies, which were observed on the following day.

Loving hands shrouded the casket in which he lay with "a magnificent national banner of silk; over the head lay a well-earned chaplet of classic laurel, on the breast a large wreath of evergreen and white flowers, in the centre of which appeared a single white floral star, and at the foot a beautiful cross formed of the same pure white material."

At half-past one the body was transferred from the Planters' House to the Second Baptist Church, where as a mere youth, on entering that city years before, he first found a home in the public worship of God.

At the church, in front of the altar, a beautiful arch of evergreens and white flowers had been arranged with great taste, and underneath it his coffin was placed by those who had loved him faithfully in life.

The religious exercises were conducted in the presence of a very large and attentive audience, in a most solemn and impressive manner, by Dr. Post and the Rev. J. P. Schofield.

At the close of the service the choir sung Montgomery's beautiful hymn,

" Go to the grave in all thy glorious prime,
    In full activity of zeal and power."

"At the conclusion of the religious services the body was received by the military escort, consisting of the Ninety-first Illinois Infantry, Lieutenant-Colonel Smith commanding, and two squadrons of the Fourth Regular Cavalry, the entire escort commanded by Colonel Day.

" The cortege moved with slow and measured tread, led by Boehm's splendid band, thundering the awful notes of a grief-inspiring requiem, which, as it swelled to a perfect diapason, embodied at once the prayers and sorrow for the dead.

"Along the streets traversed by the cortege the sidewalks were lined in many parts with citizens, for the people loved the name of General Boomer for the bravery and goodness he was animated with in his lifetime; and as the boat pushed out

from the wharf, transporting his honored dust from
the soil of his adoption forever, many a sigh went
up, and tears were shed from eyes all 'unused to
the melting mood.'"

General Boomer's remains were conveyed to
the home of his father, in Worcester, Mass., for
interment, and it was the design of his family to
quietly place them in their final resting-place.
But the loyal citizens of Worcester remonstrated
against this plan, and strongly urged that *they*
might have an opportunity of showing their gratitude, in a public way, to one who had so generously suffered and died to maintain a common
cause. This wish being acceded to, every honor
was most generously paid to the dead by the kind
hearts of that city.

On Sunday, the 28th June, his funeral obsequies
were observed in Worcester, at the Third Baptist
Church.

Long before the hour of service the church was
filled to its utmost capacity.

The religious exercises on this occasion were
conducted with great earnestness and sympathy
by the Rev. J. Banvard.

"He gave a brief sketch of the more prominent
points in General Boomer's career, and paid a

merited tribute to his eminent worth, closing with
an urgent appeal to the men of the North to rise
in the majesty of their whole might, to crush out
the rebellion, and save their country, for which so
much blood had already been shed."

This deeply interesting service was closed by
the chanting of that exquisitely tender hymn, —

" Into the silent land, ah ! who shall lead us thither ? "

The casket which contained the remains of the
deceased was again draped with the national banner, again profusely decked with bouquets and
wreaths of flowers, and escorted to their last repose, in the Rural Cemetery, by the State Guards
and the Highland Cadets, accompanied by the
Worcester Cornet Band.

The throngs that crowded the streets to pay
their last tribute of respect to the memory of him
who in his turn had passed into " the silent halls
of death," gave an affecting testimony to the fact
that the great heart of the North beat in sympathy
with the honest soldier.

But he to whom these honors were paid had
passed beyond the reach of human praise. His
work was done, his voice was silenced, his eye ob-
scured, his arm paralyzed, — but not until they
had each and all been uplifted for the cause he

loved: not until he had done something for the progress of the world's civilization, in which he felt a deep interest.

On the death of such a man, the patriot and the friend might justly pause to shed a tear, and say with truth, —

> " His life was gentle, and the elements
> So mixed in him that Nature might stand up
> And say to all the world, — This was a man ! "

In this hour of our country's gloom, when clouds roll on clouds, when woes cluster on woes, when every cup is full of bitterness, every prospect is draped in black, how precious the record of such lives ! This gigantic rebellion furnishes an innumerable host, to be gathered from every camp and hospital and battle-field.

How delicious the fragrance of such unfading memories ! How full of consolation such imperishable legacies !

The spirit of these " fallen braves " shall never die. " It shall outlive the ruins of empires and of eras, and, passing through the web of time, it will weave the bright colors of virtue, self-denial, and loyalty to God and liberty, into the mighty fabric of human souls, which shall be unrolled at the judgment, and then hung up as the golden tapestry of heaven."

One of the most brilliant pages of history records the fact that the world-renowned Cæsar, "in dying, first gazed on the marble brow of Pompey, and then arranged his robes to lie with becoming dignity in death." On another page, of equal lustre, the record is made of Nelson, before his last battle,—Trafalgar,— saying, "Now for a peerage or Westminster Abbey!" But how much loftier and purer the spirit of our brave warriors, who, with an entire abnegation of self, accept the most trying agonies of death upon our battle-fields, knowing that their names and deeds will be alike unknown to history or to fame!

"In that wreath which a grateful nation twines around *her* brow, the most brilliant and imperishable flowers will be those gathered from the hallowed graves of the men who have freely offered up their lives on the altar of their country."

But a far more enduring and glorious reward awaits our Christian soldiers than that bestowed upon them by any earthly homage. Passing through the dark river of death, they are bidden to enter the pearly gates of the New Jerusalem, whose foundations are built of precious stones. In that better country there are no envyings, no strifes, no wars nor rumors of wars. The mild reign of

23

the Prince of Peace beams over all, and transplanted to those everlasting gardens of God's love, where angels walk, angelic hands shall crown their spotless brows with unfading diadems.

CHAPTER XIV.

TESTIMONIALS.

FROM the many testimonials by General Boomer's friends in St. Louis, the following extracts are made: —

" General Boomer came to this city when a mere youth, with a business upon his hands that required the judgment, good sense, and experience of mature years. These traits of character he soon developed in an extraordinary degree, and by them he won the confidence of all who had business connections with him. He took at once an enviable position as a man of integrity and real worth, — a position which he always maintained.

. . . .

"It was evident to all who knew our dear departed Boomer, that he was governed by no common aims in life, — that he had a high standard of manliness, ripened by much thought and reflection. One of the prominent traits of his character was his justice. Whatever he said he would do, he did. No one doubted his motives, or believed that they were covered by any cloak of policy, or that any selfish end was sought. He was unflinching in his principles, but kind in maintaining them; just and generous, the soul of honor and truth. These traits made him greatly beloved, because he could be entirely trusted.

.   .   .   .

" General Boomer possessed the highest order of talents, and rarely has any young man, thrown into a world of strangers dependent upon himself, accomplished what he did. He won a reputation, both in this city and in the country where he was known, that no man of his years has ever excelled or equalled in the State of Missouri. So great was his popularity in the country, that it was the wish of the people in the district to which his town of Castle Rock belonged to send him as their representative to Washington.

.   .   .   .

" In the death of this brave soldier the State of Missouri has lost one of its brightest gems. He was a young man whose high-toned moral character, whose activity and enterprise, whose ambition to use his time and talents to the best possible advantage, were well worthy the imitation of our young men. All who knew him loved him, for they believed in him. He had a keen knowledge of character, was sound in judgment, always kind and magnanimous.

"Too much cannot be said in praise of the brilliant record he has left behind, and although he lived but few years, yet it was a long life in noble deeds and manly action. The people of Missouri will long love and honor his name."

"OSAGE CITY, MISSOURI, July 10, 1863.

"I have been intimately acquainted with the late General Boomer for the last six years, and have always been advised of the estimation in which he was held in the community. His acquaintance was extensive, and among all his numerous business connections in the country he was always regarded as a man of sterling and unswerving integrity.

"Since the breaking out of the rebellion his popularity has greatly extended and increased, through the universal attachment and devotion of the members of the Twenty-sixth Regiment, whose letters to their friends at home have been filled with descriptions of the sayings and doings of their noble commander. One old gentleman, living in this place, whose son was a captain in the Twenty-

23*

sixth Regiment, shed tears upon reading the announcement of General Boomer's death.

"There has never been any man in this community who was so universally beloved and esteemed, nor any one whose loss could be so generally felt or so deeply regretted as his."

" CASTLE ROCK, September 18, 1863.

" As a man of business in this place, General Boomer pleased and satisfied all with whom he had any transactions. He was remarkable in possessing the desirable faculty of pleasing every one, on account of his justness and kindness. Free from excitement, generous to a fault, energetic, and given to detail in his business relations, manly and considerate, he was beloved by all who knew him.

.   .   .   .

" All who knew Boomer loved him. There was a strength and tenderness in his nature that made him a universal favorite wherever he went. He was noble, generous, and true, and his loss falls heavily upon the people of this community. It will never be made up to them."

" BEFORE VICKSBURG, June 14, 1863.

" MY DEAR MRS. S——: Though no words of mine can assuage the grief or fill the place made vacant by the loss of a dearly loved brother, still it is with a feeling of pride that I can bear testimony to his exalted character, his signal ability, and his patriotic devotion to his country, for the sake of which he lost his life in an attempt to storm this stronghold of the enemy on the twenty-second ult.

" Though he has been taken from us, his spirit still lives and animates his surviving comrades, — ' it can never die.'

" While he was my friend and companion in arms, he was more than a friend, — he was a support, one in whom I placed the greatest confidence, and whom I had learned to love as a brother.

" The last written communication I had from him was the day before the assault, in which he said he had discovered a good route leading nearly up to the enemy's works, where troops could be marched under cover from their fire. I went down, and we talked the matter over, examined the grounds, and concluded the plan was feasible. The next morning he led his column to the assault; but before the final assault was made, the Seventh Division, to which he belonged, was sent to the assistance of General McClernand, who had asked General Grant for reinforcements, and it was in front of his lines that he lost his life.

"Very sincerely your friend,

"J. P. McPherson,

"*Major-General.*"

"Rochester, N. Y., June 26, 1863.

"Mrs. S——.

"My dear Madam: I saw and conversed with your brother and my friend several times on the sad and eventful day when he gave his life for the country which he had served so long and so well. Though exposed the whole day, he was unharmed until my division was detached from General McPherson's and ordered to the support of General McClernand's corps, in the afternoon. The three brigades of the division were then sent to different points, and I was not near your brother when he fell, but one of his aids reported the event to me soon after it occurred. He had formed his brigade to make a charge on the enemy's works, and was instantly killed as he was moving forward to give the final orders.

"I saw his body just before dark, after it had been brought from the field, and was impressed by the natural and composed posture and expression of the face. There was no distortion, and but little disfigurement, so that it was difficult to persuade myself that he was really dead, and not sleeping after the fatigue of the day.

"My acquaintance with General Boomer began in the early part of December last, and from that time up to the moment we were called to mourn his loss, he was in command of the Third Brigade of my division. A better man and a braver officer, a more warm-hearted and disinterested friend, in short, a more noble man than he, I have yet to find. I conceived for him the strongest friendship from my first acquaintance, which was strengthened and cemented by an unreserved social and official intercourse.

"While it must be gratifying to you to know the high estimate in which your brother was held, and it may perhaps somewhat soften your sorrow, it cannot console you for his loss; nor do I presume that my own sorrow and heartfelt sympathy will do much to lessen your affliction.

"I regret that it was impossible to comply with your brother's wishes,—to have his remains, in the event of his death, sent to you. The attempt was made by his aid-de-camp, but he was compelled to bury them at the landing on the Yazoo

River, with the intention of forwarding them as
soon as possible.

"I am, madam, with much sympathy and respect,

"Truly your friend,

"J. F. QUIMBY."

The following is an extract from a letter of
C. A. Dana : —

"VICKSBURG, May 30, 1863.

"I have met with few persons in life for whom I
have felt such an instinctive sympathy as Boomer.
He was brave, manly, affectionate, and sincere,
keen in perception and sound in judgment. Of
the many good soldiers who have fallen in this
magnificent campaign, his death is the only one
which has caused me direct personal sorrow."

From General Crocker : —

"ST. LOUIS, June 5, 1863.

"It is due to the memory of General Boomer to
say, that there was no man of any rank in the
whole army of the Tennessee more universally beloved than he. No officer has been more conspicuous than he in this magnificent campaign, and no
generalship has excelled that which he displayed
at Champion Hills. To him, in a great measure,
we owe that victory. No man was rising so fast

in distinction as Boomer, and no death has been more generally deplored than his."

From a soldier in the Third Brigade, Seventh Division, Seventeenth Army Corps : —

" VICKSBURG, May 30, 1863.

"Alas! our beloved Boomer has fallen! He had been fighting all day, and late in the afternoon was sent to reinforce McClernand, and instead of being kept as a reserve he was ordered to the front ranks. He said to a friend that he thought this unjust : but still he obeyed every order, and cheerfully went in to take charge of his column in person.

" Just as he had drawn up his troops in line of battle, a bullet from the enemy's sharp-shooters pierced his head, killing him instantly, just as the sun was setting.

" He was the moving spirit of the division, the bravest of the brave, and has · gained an imperishable renown.' "

" WALNUT HILLS, NEAR VICKSBURG, May 28, 1863.

.   .   .   .

" But our sky is not cloudless. Dark shadows have cast their gloom over our hearts: the darkest was the death of poor Boomer.

"I cannot tell *you* what he was,— you knew and loved him so well,— but I can tell you that his loss is more generally deplored than that of any officer who has fallen in this campaign.

"On our march to Hard Times I was with him most of the way, and our intimacy increased until I felt towards him like a brother. Personally I could almost feel the bullet in my heart that pierced his head.

"He died at the head of his brigade, with his face to the foe.

"Vicksburg would be bought at a heavy price if no other life than his was paid.

"W. S. HILLYER,

"*General Grant's Staff.*"

"HEAD-QUARTERS 7TH BRIGADE,

7TH DIVISION, 17TH ARMY CORPS,

VICKSBURG, July 27, 1863.

"MRS. S——.

"DEAR MADAM: Had I known positively your name and address, I should have done myself the honor of writing you a letter of condolence at the time of your brother's death, knowing as I did, from his own remarks, that you were more to him than any other living being.

"It is indeed true that I am familiar with his military career, and it is all bright and all glorious; so that it would be a most difficult task to recite facts or incidents that would have peculiar significance or interest. His whole life as a soldier, and all the incidents of it, seem equally interesting.

" His mind was adapted to the service in every respect; and when he knew what movements our army was about to make, he was never at a loss to know what the movements of the enemy would be. For three long and tedious campaigns, namely, against Corinth, against Vicksburg by the Central Mississippi Railroad, and against Vicksburg by the river, comprising almost every variety of movement and strategy, all of which were discussed and considered, no movement was made the effect and result of which he did not exactly foretell before it was commenced.

" When a large portion of our army below Corinth was sent forward to General Buell in Cincinnati last summer, I recollect how confident he was that we should be attacked on that line at an early day. You will remember how soon the battles of Iuka and Corinth followed.

" Again, last December, when we were below Oxford, on the Tuscony Patafyty River, he constantly discussed the great danger we were in of having our supplies cut off by a raid upon the road,

24

and came one day to request me to go with him
to Grant's head-quarters and urge the necessity
of the army being supplied immediately with
twenty or thirty days' rations of hard bread and
coffee, so that, in case the road was destroyed, the
army could march on down to Vicksburg and open
communication by river, and thus no delay be in-
curred in reducing the place by any movement of
the enemy in the rear. Subsequent events, which
came speedily upon us, proved how well founded
his opinions were.

"When the last spring campaign opened we
were ordered to land about fifteen miles above
Lake Providence, and open a way for boats above
Bayou Macon, with the view of going through to
Red River to reinforce General Banks at Port
Hudson, and clearing the river as far up as War-
renton. The distance to be travelled through
these narrow, crooked bayous and small rivers,
through the enemy's country, would have been at
least four hundred miles. Your brother at once
took the most decided stand against the programme,
and when the division gave the usual military
reason for carrying it out, namely, ' that it was so
ordered,' he went so far as to say that such
orders must not be obeyed until a full consultation
was had upon them, and the whole matter recon-

sidered. He immediately took a boat and went in person to Lake Providence, to have a private interview with General McPherson on the subject, and impressed him so strongly with the insurmountable obstacles to a successful campaign thus ordered, that the General made a trip to Young's Point to see General Grant on the subject, and the whole plan was dropped.

"We were ordered down the Tallahatchie River by the Yazoo Pass, which was also a movement in which your brother had no confidence, and he often remarked, before we sailed, that the campaign would be immensely expensive, and result in no advantage to the Government; and so it proved.

"But when the last movement was commenced, by way of Brunisburg, he was filled with confidence and hope, and often remarked that he could foresee its certain success.

"In battle your brother conducted himself with as much calculation, deliberation, and calmness, as in the most common occurrences and affairs of life, and he dared to do what he saw clearly was best without orders, and even against orders in an unquestionable case.

"At the battle of Iuka, after the enemy's skirmishers were drawn back to the main line by a portion of his regiment and a fire received from nearly the whole line of the enemy, Boomer applied to me for an order to bring in his skirmishers at once, to form the whole regiment into line of battle, and be ready for an advance of the enemy, which was evidently about being made. I told him my orders from General Rosecrans were, to have the skirmishers hold their line, or advance if possible, and bring the whole body of infantry forward to their support. He said the line the skirmishers were on could not be maintained a moment, and if I did not choose to take the responsibility of ordering the skirmishers in, he would bring them in without orders, and accordingly did so; and I obtained an order to the same effect while he was doing this. Hardly had a moment elapsed after he accomplished this before the whole line of the enemy came forward like a tempest, and almost swept away the imperfect formation we had made.

"Your brother was not overcome at all or disquieted by this shock, his regiment being in reserve, and he, having full discretion as to the point where and the time when he should move, personally led to the front line, where it was most weakened, and where the fire was most destructive, with four of his best companies; and seeing at a glance that all our reserve forces were needed there, he attempted to bring them up. While doing this he was shot, and fell, as was then sup-posed, mortally wounded.

"While laboring under the pains of what he supposed, with all his friends (except his surgeon), was a mortal wound, his courage and spirit did not fail, and he was only anxious for the issue of the battle. His only regret was that he was not able to complete the movement he had commenced, which he felt confident would have relieved the whole line in a great degree.

"At Jackson, Champion Hills, and before Vicks-burg, he exhibited the same judgment, calmness, determination, and zeal. He was following my brigade to the right of our line at Champion Hills, when he received an order to move back quickly and support General Hovey's division, then being engaged and overwhelmed by superior numbers in the centre. It was but a few minutes before the whole centre of the enemy's line was falling back before him.

"The enemy was speedily reinforced at that point, and even commenced driving back the thinned ranks of Colonel Boomer's brigade. He came to me and spoke as calmly and coolly as on any occasion, saying, 'Sanborn, the enemy are too strong for my brigade where I am, but with two more regiments I can clear that part of the field.

Can't you let me have the Fifty-ninth and Forty-eighth Indiana from your brigade?' When I assured him that my troops were all engaged, but that the Second Brigade was close up, and I had heard General Grant order it at once to his support, he responded, 'That is all I want,' and rode off as cheerfully as if it were a holiday.

"In less than a half hour that part of the field was cleared, and clearing that really cleared the whole; so that your brother performed a most conspicuous part in that battle.

"When the general order was given for the army to assault the enemy's works on the 22d May, Boomer was disposed to favor it, and to believe it would be successful, and not attended with very heavy loss. He based this belief on the fact that the enemy had been recently defeated in several engagements, and was consequently demoralized, and would not make a strong stand.

"But after the movement had commenced, and the condition as well as disposition of the enemy became apparent, he had no confidence of our success, and became much depressed. This depression did not seem to be the result of any gloomy forebodings about himself, but of a fear — well founded, I think — that the assault would be carried too far, that we should lose the strength and flower of our army, and as a consequence Vicksburg, which we were sure to capture and reduce by delay.

" Later than twelve o'clock that day he told me he had become convinced that we could not gain the parapets without more than fifty per cent. of our men; that this would leave the enemy the larger force, which would be fresh, while ours would be exhausted and worn out, and that we had no chance of success. He asked me once if I did not think some one of us should go and see General McPherson in regard to the matter, and try to have the men ordered back to the camps. This, however, was but a few moments before we received a dispatch from General McClernand, saying that he was in part possession of the enemy's works; that if he could be supported he could carry the position, etc., and an order for us to move to his support.

" As we left our positions to go to the support of McClernand, I saw your brother for the last time alive. He gave a broad, full smile, such as you know he could give, which seemed to say, ' I don't believe a word of the dispatch, but am willing to go and see how it is.'

" A half hour afterwards we were both warmly engaged with the enemy in our new positions, when your brother was killed. He fell at the time of his greatest usefulness, and when moving most rapidly forward in the pathway of glory. In his case how speedily it led to the tomb!

> ' The decree went forth, and the arrow sped
> By fate's irrevocable doom;
> And the gallant young hero lies low with the dead;
> But the halo of glory that encircles his head
> Remains uneclipsed by the tomb.'

"Your brother will never be forgotten by his companions in arms; and we all, even before we could realize that we should see him in the flesh nevermore, in heart exclaimed, ' Wise counsellor! Brave soldier! Genial and faithful friend! Hail! and farewell!'

" Very truly yours,

" J. B. SANBORN,

" *Brigadier-General.*"

Made in the USA
Middletown, DE
04 December 2022

17000674R00170